Forgotten Wings

When we remember our wings,
we begin to fly

Forgotten Wings

When we remember our wings,
we begin to fly

Dawn Henderson

BOOKS

Winchester, UK
Washington, USA

First published by O-Books, 2010
O Books is an imprint of John Hunt Publishing Ltd., The Bothy, Deershot Lodge, Park Lane, Ropley,
Hants, SO24 0BE, UK
office1@o-books.net
www.o-books.com

For distributor details and how to order please visit the 'Ordering' section on our website.

A CIP catalogue record for this book is available from the British Library.

Design: Stuart Davies

Printed in the UK by CPI Antony Rowe
Printed in the USA by Offset Paperback Mfrs, Inc

We operate a distinctive and ethical publishing philosophy in all
areas of its business, from its global network of authors to
production and worldwide distribution.

CONTENTS

Heartfelt and full of good chi!
Barefoot Doctor

This lovely book will help you reconnect with who you really are -
beyond all fear and limitations - and remember how to fly.
Gill Edwards, Living Magically, Stepping into the Magic; Wild
Love; Life is a Gift

Dawn has her finger on the pulse of our current evolution. Many
people are channeling this important information and we need to listen.
A great, accessible manual to change.
Michele Knight, psychic, astrologer, broadcaster and writer:
Touched by Evil (Sunday Times best seller)

I whole-heartedly enjoyed and recommend Dawn Henderson's
Forgotten Wings. Dawn writes as a wise and compassionate fellow
traveller along the journey of spiritual awakening. She shares profound
and yet simple wisdom and guidance that is practical and most impor-
tantly, achievable. I believe her book will be a valuable companion and
way-shower for many people on their own journey of awakening to
remembering the wholeness of who they really are.
Dr Jude Currivan, cosmologist, planetary healer and author.
www.judecurrivan.com

Acknowledgements

My heartfelt thanks to John Hunt and everyone at O-Books who have made this book – and my dream – a reality.

My love and deepest thanks too to my support team – to all my friends and workshop clients – I couldn't have done it without you.

And particularly my Soul friends: Gill, Anne, Karen, Lesley and Tina for being there; for listening, supporting and encouraging me throughout this journey

To my children, Jenny and Matt, just for being you – and for being proud of me.

To Nigel: my best friend, sounding board, mirror and teacher. We have both learnt and grown so much from knowing each other. Thank you beyond words for your friendship, love, support and unwavering belief in me, especially during those times when my own belief in myself went into hiding.

To everyone who has given me such useful feedback on the various stages and drafts of Forgotten Wings and especially to Nina, Gill and Nigel: my grateful thanks for your time and help in reading over the final manuscript and for your insightful comments and suggestions.

FORGOTTEN WINGS

Someone gave me a gift today.
I whispered 'Thank You'
I held it to my heart
And I heard it speak.
In gentle words of wisdom it showed me
All that I could do
All that I could have
All that I could be
And it showed me all that I already am.
Surrounded by light
It sang me a song
And as its soft voice filled my world
I felt a stirring;
A trembling, fluttering unfurling
Of my long-forgotten
Now remembered
Wings

Dawn Henderson 2007

Preface

I find myself walking up a rocky mountain path. It is a lovely day – blue skies, candyfloss clouds and snow on the mountain tops. It is an easy path to walk and I am thoroughly enjoying myself. I climb and climb, higher and higher, and finally I emerge onto a small grassy plateau high on the mountainside. The edge falls away in an almost vertical drop of many hundreds of feet and the view is magnificent. I can see snow-capped mountains stretching away endlessly into the distance, dark mysterious forests and rocky outcrops, while here and there a distant mountain stream or waterfall glitters like molten silver in the sunlight.

I walk to the edge of the precipice and open my arms to embrace the beauty of the landscape. It takes my breath away. It feels like the world in its entirety is spread out in front of me.

I hear the voice of my spirit Guide behind me. "This is all yours," he says. "You can have the world if you wish." I turn to face him. "Yes, I do wish, oh how much I wish," I tell him "but I don't know how to reach it." "Trust and believe," comes the answer. "Just step off the edge and allow yourself to fly."

But when I turn back, I find that the edge has disappeared. I don't know how to get back to it and I don't even know how to step off it if I do find it again. I feel heartbroken. "You already have all that you need," my Guide tells me kindly. "You have your wings. You have just forgotten how to use them. When you are ready to fly, you will know how."

For many months this same message came to me in inner journeys time and time again. Always I longed to take that leap and fly. And always I couldn't. I just didn't know how.

Until...

A couple of years ago I attended a wonderfully inspirational workshop in the Lake District. Shortly after I returned home, I found myself on another inner journey, re-running the same scenario – with one major difference. This time, I didn't look around. I walked straight to the edge of the precipice, fearlessly, joyfully spread my arms and, with a whoop of delight, I leapt... and soared into the skies. I travelled to the stars and back that day. I had finally re-discovered my wings. That gift inspired me to write this book.

In Forgotten Wings I would like to share with you the personal understandings and truths I have gained from my own exciting and me changing twelve year voyage of discovery. There is so much left for me to explore, much more than there is time, either in this lifetime or in many more to come. But I believe that I am at last beginning to shake out my wings and open them to the sunlight. They are sometimes still a little stiff and rusty. And yes, there are times when it takes effort to shake them open and spread them to the light. Sometimes too they get stuck. But each time I use them it gets a little easier, a little more natural. It will take more time yet before my wings become truly part of me. But now I know they are there. And for now, that is enough. The rest will follow.

With love, light & lots of laughter,
Dawn, Summer 2009

Power thought
Your wings will take you to places beyond your wildest dreams

---

Part I
OUR FORGOTTEN WINGS

Introduction

Does it ever seem like you are sleepwalking through your life, rarely feeling truly alive? That there must be more to life than you are currently experiencing? Or that somehow you are missing the point but don't quite know why? Maybe you have shut away your dreams and longings into a dark little corner because you don't believe you can ever fulfil them? If so, you are not alone.

Most people today are living OK but limited lives in various degrees of contentment, depending on how they view the world, and believing that this is as good as it can get. How wrong can we be! We have no idea of how good it can really get. There is more to life and living than we could ever conceive. Yet we constrain ourselves within self-imposed boundaries, our lives squashed into cramped little boxes that bear no relation to how things could be, of how they are intended to be. The Life has gone out of our lives.

But if we are living in a box, it is because we have put ourselves there. No-one and no thing is stopping us soaring out of it – except ourselves. Oh, we can come up with plenty of good reasons why we can't get out (and believe me, I'm a past master at it!) - our current circumstances or our background, our race, age or sex, the economic climate. Just about anything you can think of. These though are just excuses, and none are valid. We are firmly stuck in our boxes because of the limitations and constraints we have put on ourselves. Limitations and constraints created through our learned beliefs, fears, patterns and expecta-tions. Because we take on board other peoples' beliefs and expec-tations of what we can and can't – or should and shouldn't! – do.

If your life is basically how you want it and you would simply like to deepen the love, joy and 'aliveness' within it, then this book is for you. Equally, if you feel that nothing in your life is working and you can't see a solution, it is also for you. In Forgotten Wings I offer you 10 simple keys to opening up to the incredible and infinite potential of life. Potential for a life filled with love, inner peace, joy and fulfilment (which are, after all, at the foundation of all our other desires). But also for all the other wonderful and fun-filled gifts that make life so rich and exciting: good health, prosperity, rewarding work and loving relationships. And yes, maybe even that Aston Martin, cottage by the sea or Himalayan trek.

You will learn that you *can* stop doing things just because you believe you should be doing them and instead do those things that fill you with joy. That you *can* let go of other peoples' expectations and demands to follow your own heart. That you are truly free – free to love, free to follow your dreams, free to release all the obstacles standing in your way and to live your life the way you want it. Most importantly, you will learn that you are free to be as happy as you decide to be – and that no-one and nothing else has any power over that.

This book is not a To Do list of activities aimed at bringing a specific 'something' into your life overnight. Rather, it offers ideas and suggestions that will allow you to gradually change your perception and understanding of life – and of yourself – on every level. They will help you remember who you really are, beneath all the layers and identities you have taken on over the course of your lifetime. And who you really are is your True Self, your Soul. The more we strengthen this bond with our True Self, the more we become aware of the aliveness of life, of the infinite possibilities available to us and of the freedom that has always been ours.

Neither is it an overnight quick fix. These are the conscious steps into an exciting awe-filled journey that will last your lifetime and longer. It takes time and awareness to alter your lifelong habits and beliefs, plus a real desire for change. If you are embarking on this adventure because you feel you should, or because someone else wants you to, you may as well stop reading now. You are unlikely to make much progress if these are your reasons. You can only create lasting change when you truly desire it for yourself.

It isn't complicated. The processes are simple – though not necessarily easy, as they contrast strongly with how we have been taught to think and be. It involves turning everything you believe about life and how it works on its head and throwing out all the old beliefs you have learned about what is 'right' and what is 'wrong', what is possible and what is not. And then re-establishing your own new truths, based on your personal experiences and deep inner knowing. It means becoming a maverick, not following the herd and going against accepted (and expected!) 'shoulds' and 'cans'. It may well cause frowns, unease and perhaps even conflict with other people who would much prefer you not to rock the boat or who want you to remain your old familiar self, however unhappy you are in that role.

You will need to become aware of yourself, your thoughts and how you react to things. You will need to consciously choose something different. However, in time (and usually not very much) it will become second nature, your everyday all-the-time way of being. Please come to this book and these ideas with an attitude of exploration and fun. The more you can experience it as a game, undertaken with playful curiosity, the more you will gain from it. Heavy 'should do it' thoughts will weaken your connection, so if you start feeling this way, put it away for another day and go and do something you want to do instead.

To change your life, nothing outside of you needs to change first. When you change on the inside, when you change your thoughts, beliefs, feelings and actions, your outer circumstances have to follow. You don't have to be perfect. It doesn't matter if you 'get it wrong' (actually, as we'll see, you can't). As with everything, the more you practise, the easier it gets – and the better at it you get.

On our journey through Forgotten Wings, we will be remembering many ways of thinking, of being and of seeing ourselves and the world around us. Ways that seem new but that are as old as existence. They are the ways in which our True Self, our Soul, lives. I say remembering because, while it may all seem different (and maybe even a bit radical, weird or downright whacky at times) I am not telling you anything you do not already know. You have just forgotten that you know it.

As you explore this book, please open your heart and your mind. Much of it may feel familiar to you, in which case your wings are already beginning to unfurl. Or you may not connect with it at all, and that's OK too. My aim is not to prescribe a rigid, one-size-fits-all belief system but merely to lay my reality and my truths before you, based on my personal experiences and understandings. Take what resonates with you, even if it is just a sentence, and discard the rest. I simply invite you to share my way of opening yourself to the incredible light and love of the Universe, of reconnecting with your Soul and of soaring to your dreams. To help you, Forgotten Wings is sprinkled with what I have called 'Power Thoughts' - thoughts, quotes and affirmations for you to use as your own launch pad into a new way of being.

Each person who reads this book will do so on his or her own individual frequency and will take something different from it. Every one of us is on a unique voyage of personal and spiritual growth and each of us is at a different point on that voyage. But please know that if you have picked up this book, you are already on that wonderful magical journey and that somewhere within its pages is a message for you.

(Note: I have used 'Source' and the 'Universe' interchangeably throughout Forgotten Wings as to me, they represent the same all-embracing creative power)

POWER THOUGHT

If you always think what you've always thought, you'll
always get what you've always got

What we have forgotten...

Once upon a time, before we entered our flesh and bone body to be born into and experience this physical existence we call life, we knew many, many things:

~ We knew that we are always connected to Source (or All That Is, or God, or the Universe or however else you care to name it) and that, no matter what we do, this connection can never be broken. We are Source and Source is us.

~ We knew that Source is everywhere and always and that everything that exists is a creation of Source.

~ We knew that everything created by Source (which *is* everything) is perfect, whole and sacred – and this includes ourselves.

~ We knew that Source is infinitely loving and creative and that, no matter what happens, we are safe and loved.

~ We knew that, whilst we are all unique individuals, each one of us is connected to each and every other one of us. We knew that each individual 'me' is an integral part of the magnificent whole.

~ We knew that life is our choice, our decision to experience a physical existence with all its emotions, contrasts and sensations.

~ We knew that, as part of this game of life, we would create every experience, everything we desire through our preferences, thoughts and feelings.

~ And we knew that, as each one of us is a part of the whole that is Source, we each possess the power, love and creativity of Source and can use it in exactly the same way.

This knowledge, that once we knew and have long forgotten, created the glorious shimmering wings that came with us as we entered this physical world. We were filled with unlimited potential, bursting with excitement and anticipation at this wonderful adventure. Our wings would enable us to fly to the highest heights, to reach our fullest potential and to achieve all our heartfelt dreams and desires.

We all come into this world equipped with these beautiful, shining all-powerful wings. As babies they are always with us, unfurled and ready to carry us forward. As babies the world is our oyster. We live in joy, fully in the present, slowly getting used to this marvellous physical existence. Yet as we emerge from infancy, slowly, little by little, we become more and more distanced from our True Self and our wings glow less brightly. We begin to forget who we are and where we have come from. We forget why we are here.

The outside world, the 'reality' in which we live, starts to bind our wings and our knowing. Our parents, our teachers, our societies and cultures bombard us with their truths, so different from those we have brought with us, which they have long since forgotten. And we absorb these messages. We come to see our heart-known truths as 'wrong'. We conform to others' demands and expectations. We see ourselves at the mercy of nature, other people or events. Perhaps even worse, we may believe we are being watched, judged and punished by God.

We grow up taking in these sorts of messages daily. Perhaps we learn that we are mere pawns in the hands of Fate and cannot do anything to change our lot. Or that the world is a dangerous place to be and that it isn't safe to stand out, to be different, to take risks. Or that, no matter what we do, we cannot change our destiny. We come to see ourselves as powerless. Perhaps there are *some* things we can change but when it comes to the serious stuff – don't even think about it! Our wings slowly fade and become invisible. By the time we are teenagers they are just a distant memory and by adulthood most of us have completely forgotten their existence.

We forget our dreams – or at best sit them on a high shelf to look at and dust now and again, to sigh over and believe impossible. We forget who we truly are and what life is for. We become locked in a world based on other people's experiences and expectations of reality rather than our own, their realities based primarily on fear, guilt and struggle. We forget that love is all that is really real. We remain caterpillars, crawling on the ground while gazing at the glorious skies above and wishing we could fly free, forgetting those perfect wings that would allow us to do so.

Happily, there are some people who do not forget. When you meet someone who is healthy, happy and abundant in all things, open your eyes, open your heart and look for their wings – they are using them, whether they know it or not.

For most of us, however, our wings lie dry, dusty and sleeping, hidden from our senses and our memory. Yet, somewhere, somehow, we know they do still exist. We strive, often unsuccessfully, to make our hopes and dreams come true. We struggle and effort, blame and judge, criticise and anger, seeking that elusive something we know is missing. And still, more often than not, our deepest desires and true happiness elude us. In vain our Soul nudges us to shake our wings free, to spread and warm them in the sunshine. But we cannot get them to unfurl – because we don't remember how.

It is so easy, in our sleeping, forgetting state, to see ourselves as nothing more than flesh and bone creatures inhabiting a piece of rock, albeit a beautiful piece of rock, that floats around somewhere in space and existing only for the time of that physical experience. Yet we are so much more. When we remember the truth about ourselves, when we remember that we are eternal and that this life is only one of many, many such experiences, we start to rediscover our wings. To recognise just how powerful we are. We remember that we have the ability to change our lives into heaven on Earth. And here is where heaven

9

has always been, we just haven't seen it or allowed it to be. When we re-awaken our wings and learn how to fly with them, they will carry us to the fulfilment of our dreams, to a life filled with love, joy, health and abundance in all things. We see our own truths about who we really are, where we have come from and what life is actually all about (which may come as a big and very pleasant surprise to some of you reading this book). Life is intended to be a magical joyful journey. When we use our wings, it will be.

If all this has got you scratching your heads in bewilderment (and possibly total disbelief!), don't worry. In the following chapters we'll be exploring ways to awaken these memories, to reconnect with who we really are and at last unfold our magnificent all-powerful wings to the light.

So who are we?

Why are we here? What is this thing called life all about anyway?

Who are we?

Simply put, we are all pieces of Source. Sparks of the divine consciousness. Gods and goddesses in our own right. Nothing more and nothing less. We are eternal beings of pure energy, love and light who have chosen a physical existence in order to experience every wonderful sensation of this exciting adventure we call Life.

In our physical existence, we are three parts: body, mind and spirit. One cannot exist without the other. And yet most of us identify ourselves purely through our transient physical and mental selves. We forget and neglect our spiritual being, the part of us that carries the memory of who we truly are, that carries the memory of our power. Perhaps because it is the deepest, most mysterious and secret part of ourselves.

That deep buried, forgotten part of us is the eternal True Self, our Soul. The part of us that never dies. At the end of a physical lifetime it simply returns home from whence it came, maybe to reflect on its experiences, maybe (often) to choose to re-incarnate in order to experience more. And yet, though buried and hidden, neglected and forgotten, our Soul still makes its presence felt. We have squashed it into this flesh and blood shell, though it is so much bigger than that. And every now and again it escapes to remind us of its existence.

Think of a time when you have been in a place of breath-taking natural beauty..... gazed into the flickering flames of an open fire..... lost yourself in a baby's smile..... stopped time at lover's touch..... been taken to virtual heaven by the taste of a chocolate dessert (yes, it can happen!). At these times, we reconnect with our true nature. Our spirit swells and grows as we experience utter bliss and we feel it expanding through the limits of our physical self to fill the space around us. And this can be a huge space. What you are feeling is your Soul.

I experience this when I am walking on open moorland, the wind blowing in my hair, the endless ever-changing skies stretching out in front of me. Or dancing, lost in the music. Allowing the words to flow freely through me when I'm writing. Or watching the birds feeding in my garden. Or..... Or.....

> *This is my true home.*
> *This is my True Self.*
> *The wild untamed home of my wild untamed Soul*
> *That lies*
> *Hidden and unremembered.*
> *Deep buried beneath the busy-busy clitter-clatter of my*
> *   daily life.*
> *And I remember.*
>
> (Dawn Henderson, 2007)

We all have our special moments. Those occasions that expand our Souls to fill the world and fill our hearts so we think they will burst. We need these things. They feed us, put us back in touch with our True Self and remind us of how life is intended to be. We fully sense our power, our divinity and our connection to all things. The more we practise using our wings, the more moments like this we experience, even when life gets tough, even when things are not the way we would choose them to be. And the closer we get to reconnecting with our True Self and under-standing the reasons why we are here.

This secret part of ourselves stretches so much deeper and further than we can ever imagine. But if that's the case, what and where is it? You can give it whatever name you like – the True Self, Higher Self, Soul, Spirit, Higher Consciousness. The name doesn't matter. All these terms and more refer to that part of us that is always connected to Source, permanently linked in to the stream of love and creativity that gave birth to us, allowing it to flow constantly into and through us. It is the channel for the everlasting wellbeing that is always available to us and which is as vital to us as air, water and food. When we neglect it, we become shrivelled empty shells.

Our True Self is that part of us that knows and remembers everything. It is our divinity; the god-power within us. It exists only in unconditional love and joy and knows that, whatever we may forget whilst we are in our physical flesh and blood body, we are always loved, safe and supported. It is pure Source energy. A fragment of divine consciousness and creative power. It never forgets who we truly are, or why we are here.

We really are so much more than we know. We are amazing! When we learn to see ourselves in this way, we begin to recognise the incredible potential we all have inside us and the world suddenly becomes a more joyful, loving and magical place.

POWER THOUGHT
We are so much more than we know

We are all One

When we are born into this physical existence we quickly forget who we really are. We forget our power, our creativity and our eternal-ness. As we grow, we begin to see ourselves as individuals, separate from everyone and everything else. And of course in one sense we are individuals, with our own prefer-ences, our own characters, quirks and foibles, our own experi-ences and realities. But on another, deeper level we know that this is an illusion. We are all One, all connected. Nothing can happen to a single one of us without it impacting somewhere, at some level, on all of us. These connections are eternal and cannot be broken.

Modern physics (well, it all started with Albert Einstein) is now backing this up. At the basis of everything, whether it is a thought, a brick or an elephant, there exists ONLY energy. The whole universe is nothing but pure energy, shimmying around. If we take a look at our physical body under a powerful enough microscope, all we see is a seething mass of energy bouncing about. Everything that up until very recently we have believed to be solid is actually energy vibrating in a mass of nothingness. There is no solid 'stuff'. The difference between seemingly solid matter such as a rock and, for example, a thought, is simply the frequency at which this energy moves. The slower the vibration, the denser the matter.

So, if everything is energy, everything is made of the same stuff. And every bit of this stuff called energy is connected to every other bit of energy. Because it is connected, anything affecting one part must affect the whole. This has parallels in the Butterfly Effect of Chaos Theory, which states that a butterfly flapping its wings in the Amazon rainforest may cause a typhoon in Japan. Once we understand this connection, that we are all One, that there is no 'them' and 'us', that whatever I do to you I am also doing to myself, compassion and unconditional love become natural and inevitable.

In addition, we are all connected to Source. We are all individual sparks of pure Source energy within a great whole. We are each a part of Source and we are Source itself. As such we each have within us the same creative power that Source has. We just don't remember it. Immersed in our physical existence we have forgotten this One-ness. We get so wrapped up in the human experience that our physical consciousness and Ego take over. But our Soul has not forgotten. And it is this forgotten power that we need to remember, if we are to truly live life as it is intended. We are Source, and Source is us. When you look around at what Source has already created, simply through its desire and its intention – the stars and galaxies, this beautiful planet Earth, humankind, plants, animals, the list is endless – and then we realise that this same power is within *us*...WOW!

These connections, with each other and with Source, cannot be broken. We are each an inseparable part of a huge and magnificent One.

POWER THOUGHT

When we reconnect with our True Self we open to the magic and joy of life

---

Why are we here? What is this thing called life all about?

Life is a magical voyage of joyful discovery, experiences and creation. It is love, joy and freedom – at least, that is how it is intended to be. We move into these physical bodies to experience the delights of a physical existence. As we experience, we grow. And as we grow, Source grows with us. It has to because we are an integral part of it. And that is why we were created, to enable Source to experience through us and, as a consequence, expand. Source has imposed no restrictions on us. We are free to choose to live our lives in any way we desire. For most of us at this current time, that tends to be through struggle and fear. In life, we go exactly where we choose to go, whether consciously or unconsciously.

Life is the joy of remembering our True Self, of remembering that we are beings of pure love, light and power, of experiencing everything a physical existence has to offer us and of the process of creating every experience we have – of creating our own reality. We are here to live freely and spontaneously, grasping eagerly and with appreciation every opportunity and experience. We are free to choose to do, be and have ANYTHING we desire – no conditions.

This concept may well come as a huge relief to many people. It may also be very difficult for some people to accept as it goes against everything they have ever been taught – although maybe not against what they have always felt. It means that there is no deeper purpose or 'God-given' mission to fulfil, no karma to work through, no lessons to learn and no wrongs to right. The meaning of life is what we want it to be. There is no goal or objective, nothing to 'fix' or past bad deeds to pay for. We choose how we want our lives to be, we choose our own goals – and we choose our own meaning. No-one and no thing outside ourselves can tell us its purpose or meaning. Only we can do that.

Life is not intended to be a struggle or a trial, a punishment or penance or something to be got through before reaching heaven at its end. Life is not for 'putting right' ourselves or other people, being 'good' and obedient, serving or saving anyone or anything, including souls – we will look at all this in later chapters – or finding and fulfilling our life's purpose. None of us has been charged with a mission to accomplish. If I want to change the world, that is a life purpose, a mission, *I* have chosen. Not one I have been given. Choosing our own life purpose also means that, if we want to, we can change our mind part way through and decide to do something else instead, which I think is great – and incredibly liberating.

Our only pre-ordained purpose is to experience physical life. The means by which we choose to do so is entirely our choice. Love and joy are the easiest paths but we can choose struggle instead. No-one pre-ordains the path we choose – we make it up as we go along through our thoughts, beliefs and emotions. But if you do want to change the world, begin now to live only in love and joy, remembering who you truly are – a divine being. And by living and remembering this way we can really change the world without trying. Because when others see us living in joy and love, and see our lives blossoming as we do so, they will want to do the same. Heaven is intended to be here on Earth, right now, in this life – and in the next… and the next … and the next. All we have to do (and it's a pretty big 'All') is understand and accept this – and live our lives in this way.

Sadly, we have forgotten all of this. And even when we do catch a glimpse of it, we turn our backs on it and believe it too good to be true. But nothing is ever too good to be true. There cannot be a 'too good' as there is no limit as to how good it can get. For all of us. But we cannot conceive how good it can (and is meant to) be. Messages absorbed from our growing up, our religion, our society or the media constantly teach us that we aren't good or deserving enough. And because we believe we don't deserve all this good, we push it away. So it doesn't last. Or it has a sting in its tail. The best gift we can give ourselves is to forget all this nonsense about not deserving. To know, without any doubt, that we deserve the best in everything, simply because we exist. Allow yourself to receive it.

POWER THOUGHT

When you reach out with gratitude to receive all Life has
to give you, Life gives you more

FORGOTTEN WINGS

Part II

Awakening our wings

There are so many ways we can gently nudge our wings awake. The wonderful thing is that it really doesn't matter which one we start with. After all, as the well-known Chinese proverb says, a journey of 10,000 miles begins with just one step. Once we take that step, one by one new concepts, new teachers and new experiences present themselves to us as and when we are ready, encouraging us to travel in directions we could never previously have imagined. Little steps, taken one at a time, lead to huge changes in the way we see ourselves and life – and in the way life responds to us. We feel our wings shiver and tremble as they slowly awaken.

In Part II of Forgotten Wings I offer you 10 simple keys to remembering and awakening your own fabulous wings. It really doesn't matter which one you start with or how long it takes....

So, if you are ready to change your life, to move into a world of joy, love and freedom, if you are ready to step into your power, what are we waiting for..........

Let's Go!

Key 1

We create it all

One of the most positive and effective ways we can change our lives is to acknowledge that we are responsible, not just for our words and actions, but for *everything* we experience. We create it all. This can be hard to hear and many people refuse to accept this responsibility. They do not want to believe they have created their illness, their poverty, their unsatisfactory relationships or whatever – but on some level, and although not intentionally, they have. In fact, welcoming this as our reality is incredibly empowering. For if we have created something then we are equally capable of un-creating it – or of creating something different and more desirable.

But *how* are we responsible for this? *How* do we create it? Well, it's all down to something called the Law of Attraction.

The role of the Law of Attraction

When the DVD and book of *The Secret*[1] appeared in 2006, it caused a minor sensation. Not amongst the wisdom keepers who had long known its story but for those of us who have not travelled so far along their path it was a revelation. Its message: that we are all subject to something called The Law of Attraction, which puts us fully and solely in charge of our lives and our destiny. Not fate. Not karma. Not good or bad luck or any other outside cause. Just us.

Yet as *The Secret* tells us, this is not new wisdom. As a Universal Law, the Law of Attraction has existed since before the beginning of the universe. Its power has been understood in cultures and spiritual teachings worldwide dating back thousands of years. But it is only recently that this knowledge has been passed on to a mass audience, spreading its understanding in a way never before experienced.

The reason for looking at this area first is simple – it underpins everything else we experience in life. Once we accept and understand it, we start seeing life as our Soul does – as an opportunity to play and to experience the joy of creating something fabulous. Through its guidance, Source encourages us to reach for our dreams. Creativity is an inborn and integral part of every human being, since it is an integral and inescapable part of our Soul. Creativity is who we are and the Law of Attraction allows us to tap into it constantly.

Over the past few years a lot has been written about the Law of Attraction. Some of the material is helpful and enlightened. Some of it is, unfortunately, confusing and sometimes contradictory. Some of it is just plain misleading. Everywhere we look we find books, articles and DVDs on the subject. It comes under many headings – cosmic ordering, conscious creation, reality creation, manifesting, to name just a few. It has become big business with countless seminars, workshops and study courses on offer to teach us how to work miracles in our lives. Now I am a firm believer in our ability to create our own miracles but I can't help feeling that along the way the message has frequently become over- complicated.

It's not! The Law of Attraction is straightforward and consistent and I shall be setting out for you clearly and simply my understanding of it and how it works. We will also be looking at how, using our understanding of this Law, we can consciously and deliberately use its power to create change in our lives and manifest our dreams.

What is it ... and how does it work?
The Law of Attraction is a Universal Law, like the Law of Gravity or the Laws of Mathematics. And just like them it is functioning all the time. Every second of every minute of every day. We

cannot switch it in or off or choose when it does or doesn't affect us any more than we can switch off the Law of Gravity to stop us crashing to the ground if we fall off a ladder. The Universal Laws are totally objective and neutral and the Law of Attraction is no exception. It does not judge what is good or bad, right or wrong. Our age, race, sex, IQ score or anything else has no bearing, any more than it does when we fall off that ladder. Whether we know about it or believe in it makes no difference. It just is. Always in action.

So what does this celebrated Law do? Simply put, it states that like attracts like. What though does that mean and how does it relate to our lives?

You'll remember that everything at its most fundamental level is just energy and that everything we do, think or feel emits an energy vibration. An electrical impulse if you like. So our every thought, feeling, belief and action sends out an energy wave that has its own specific frequency (rate of vibration) that can be scientifically measured and verified. This energy wave attracts to it other energy waves on the same frequency, gradually building up into a larger wave. The more energy that combines, the greater its strength. Eventually this build-up of energy becomes so strong and powerful that its essence manifests on the physical plane – and thus in our lives. In practical terms, what this means is that when we think about something constantly (whether it is something we want or something we do *not* want) we attract matching thoughts and feelings on that wavelength. The more this happens the stronger the energy around those thoughts and feelings becomes. So we are increasingly likely to experience in our lives the things we have been thinking about.

The plus of this is that when we are focussing on something we very much desire – *and* sending out coherent vibrations through our beliefs and emotions (this is REALLY important!) – we can attract it into our lives. The downside is that because so many of us are unaware of the power of the Law of Attraction and how it works, our thoughts and feelings tend to ramble on unchecked. As a result we tend to manifest in our lives people, things and events we would prefer not to experience. Our fears, negative thoughts and judgements all have a powerful creative power.

POWER THOUGHT

Live, love, laugh... everything else will take care of itself

---

A bit about Quantum Physics

To understand how the Law of Attraction works, we are going to delve into the world of physics and more specifically *quantum physics*. If that thought sends you into a cold sweat, don't panic! I am most definitely not a physicist. Anything to do with formulae, equations or technical blurb and my normally intelligent brain turns to mush. But this stuff is actually quite straightforward and easy to grasp at the level we are looking at.

First, a little history. Up until Albert Einstein, the science of physics was based almost solely on Newtonian theories of how the world worked. Newtonian physics saw the universe as comprising solid objects drawn to each other by gravity. The atom was the smallest possible particle that existed in the universe and was also seen as solid matter. Einstein and his contemporaries blew these ideas out of the water, breaking down atoms into smaller and smaller components – neutrons, photons, quarks and electrons to name but a few. And what they discovered was that when they got down to this infinitesimal level, these tiny components weren't physical material at all. They were bits of pure energy bouncing around..

This is the field of quantum physics. But it didn't end there. Other experiments took these discoveries to a new level. As early as 1909 it was discovered that the way these minute bits of energy reacted depended on *how the observer expected them to react.* When the scientist observing them expected to see an energy wave, they acted as a wave (non-physical). When however the observer expected to see a particle, they acted as a particle (physical). In other words, when the observer expected to see a particle, the non-physical energy wave became physical matter – the particle. In 1998 a scientific report from Israel's Weiszmann Institute of Science stated that in their experiments, the more the particles were observed, the more they were affected by the observer.[2]

Once we understand that science has observed pure energy transforming into matter, through expectation and observation alone, the Law of Attraction ceases to be an airy-fairy flight of fancy and comes into the 'real' world. This is where science and magic meet. Everything becomes possible. Miracles are an every day event. And we see how and why we are the creators of our reality and how and why we are responsible for everything we experience.

POWER THOUGHT
We create it ALL

Take responsibility for your life

Sadly, most of us are either unaware of the Law of Attraction or we see it as some New Age mumbo jumbo. We have forgotten the creative power that lies within us and so we create by default – and this usually results in us manifesting lives for ourselves that are somewhat less than we would consider perfect. We blame everything else for our situation, not realising the solution is within us. When we fully accept that, deliberately or unwittingly, we have attracted everything that 'happens' to us in our lives, every moment, we take back our power. We may not like what we are getting, we may not consciously desire it, or have attracted it 'on purpose' but for some reason and on some level we have created it.

It is important to emphasise that responsibility is not the same as blame. Blame weakens and disempowers us. Responsibility strengthens and empowers us. It is response-ability – the ability to respond. When we accept responsibility we allow ourselves the opportunity to change things, to respond positively and effectively. Feeling blame just makes us feel bad. It also promotes the belief that we have failed or got it wrong, when in fact, there is no such thing as failing or getting it wrong. Everything we are experiencing fits perfectly into where we are now. Once we consciously use this, we can move forward in huge strides.

And remember, we aren't just responsible for all the unwanted, unpleasant things we create. We also generate all those wonderful, joyful, exciting events. Shakespeare wrote that 'All the world is a stage and all the men and women merely players'. Well, he was almost right. To update it a bit, all the world is a film set – and whilst we are the actors, we also write our own script and storyline - and we can change it whenever we choose.

It is through our thoughts, our beliefs and our emotions that we determine how our lives are. And the only person responsible for my thoughts, beliefs and emotions is… Me. No-one else. Yes, I can put the blame on my teachers, my parents, my spouse, my children, my society or spiritual leaders – or a thousand and one other causes - but at the end of the day no-one makes me feel the way I feel, think the way I think or believe what I believe but me. I have a choice. I always have a choice. The ultimate choice that can and will never be taken away. I can choose what I think, what I believe and how I feel. I can choose how I will act or react. We all have that power, always. No matter what our situation.

Freedom and choice

Freedom is the basis of who we are. We are free to be whoever and whatever we want. Free to choose what we believe and how we feel. Free to follow our own path and our own dreams, regardless of what anyone else wants from us. And this freedom is available to each and every one of us. We are free because we always have a choice. Granted, it doesn't always feel that way but that is because we have forgotten it.

Even when we are feeling totally trapped by circumstances, we still have conscious choices – to accept or resist, to seek out joy or to wallow in misery. Our decision determines how we experience the situation and how quickly we are able to change it. As we have seen, when we resist, mired in low frequency thoughts and feelings, the Law of Attraction brings us more of the same. Accepting how things are while focussing on a more preferable situation allows us to move forward. Sometimes these choices may be so obvious or so unthinkable that we cannot see that any alternative exists. But it does. Always. Often simply acknowledging this – just knowing that we *could*, even if we have no intention of doing so – brings us back into our power. This is our freedom.

Freedom is being able to decide how we perceive anything and everything we experience. It doesn't matter what anyone else thinks or feels, we are in total control of our own thoughts and feelings. Even when outside circumstances restrict our physical liberty, if for example we have created the experience of imprisonment, this freedom still remains.

Choose how you live your life. Rejoice that every experience is your creation, even the unwanted ones, those you would prefer not to have, for they contain great gifts if you are prepared to look for them. Everything we attract reflects our innermost beliefs and the vibrations we are emitting through those beliefs and through our thoughts and feelings. Take the time to go inside and uncover why you have created the reality you are currently experiencing. It is far more empowering and inspiring to know that the solution you seek is within you than to believe you are dependent on someone else, or that you are a helpless victim of circumstance.

POWER THOUGHT

The ultimate key to freedom is recognising that every-thing is a choice – Deepak Chopra

---

Take charge of your thoughts and emotions
Despite how it appears (and frequently feels), we can take charge of and change our thoughts and emotions. They are not in control of us, unless we allow them to be. How many of us really understand this? Understand that if we change the way we look at something, the way we feel about it has to change too?

Changing our thoughts and beliefs doesn't come easily. We (or rather, our Egos) love to be right. We stand certain that our beliefs are the one and only truth. While our beliefs do indeed create our truths, 'truth' is not set in stone, so by changing our beliefs, we change our truths.

How do we do this? By remembering that a belief is only a thought that we have had so often it has become true for us. By being fully conscious of what our thoughts are. By examining whether they serve and enhance or hinder and lessen us and, if it is the latter, by letting them go and choosing different ones. Our outer world always reflects what is within us. Changing our thoughts changes our truths, which as a consequence changes our reality. Whilst to begin with, things may not change on the outside in any concrete way, our perception of them, their 'reality' to us, *will* change.

Two people can be in an identical situation. One is upbeat, optimistic and cheerful. The other is downbeat, pessimistic and miserable. Each will view his situation in a completely different light and, as a result, the Universe will deliver to each more of what he is experiencing. So the optimist will attract things that strengthen his optimism and the pessimist will, in his turn, attract things that reinforce that he is right to be pessimistic. Both believe that theirs is the truth and both are right.

You could say that it is purely a matter of perspective. Of course... isn't everything? The optimist is choosing the perspective of positive thought, choosing to live in light and joy. The other is choosing the opposite, to live in gloom and misery. Their choice! If you had the choice (and you definitely do!), which would you choose?

POWER THOUGHT

It's purely a matter of perspective

If understanding that we are able to choose what we think and believe is challenging, accepting that we can do the same with our emotions is even more so. We see ourselves as slaves to them as we allow them to rampage on unabated, influencing everything we say, think and do. Or conversely we bury and repress them, pretending they do not exist until one day they explode out of all proportion and in a totally unwarranted situation or express themselves as some physical dis-ease.

But emotions are just a product of our thoughts, our reaction to the thoughts that are moving through us. So, by changing our thoughts, we can change our emotions. As a simple example, have you ever got really angry about some situation? Then someone points out something you hadn't considered, that makes you reassess, and your anger dissolves in an instant? You have changed your thoughts about the situation – and as a result, your emotions have changed.

This doesn't mean that we should deny or belittle our feelings. They are a vital guidance mechanism that helps us to know where we are in regard to a situation and whether we are headed in the direction we want to go. Every feeling we have is valid and an integral, natural and essential part of ourselves. Denying and repressing them, not allowing ourselves to feel them truthfully, locking them up deep inside ourselves sooner or later leads to physical dis-ease.

But it is so easy to allow ourselves to get locked into a cycle of painful emotions from which it becomes ever harder to escape. We wallow in old hurt, resentment or guilt for example so that those feelings become part of who we are. Unfortunately this stops us from ever truly living life as it is intended.

Once we have accepted and fully experienced our feelings, *as they occur*, we can choose to let them go and move on. We can choose to feel differently. We do this by consciously changing our thoughts about the situation that has created those feelings – by changing our perspective. As a simple example, say I have met a friend for coffee and it is clear that she is not in the best of moods. I make some comment and she snaps at me. I have a choice. I can take offence, feel hurt and insulted and perhaps snap back. Or I can accept I feel hurt but choose to let it pass, understanding that this grumpiness is out of character and that there is a reason why she is acting this way. It is this choice, which we always have, that makes us truly free. (Anything else is a severe case of the tail wagging the dog instead of the dog instructing his tail).

This will automatically begin to raise our energy vibrations so that finding these better-feeling thoughts becomes easier and easier. And as we attract more of these thoughts, we also attract people and experiences that reinforce them.

Of course, the process isn't always easy and it can't be rushed. Painful, powerful emotions such as grief take time to process and heal, and allowing this time is vital. But if we truly want to then slowly, in baby steps, we can move to a better feeling place.[3]

I am not saying that if we are unwell, we 'shouldn't' desire better health or if we are in an unsatisfactory relationship, that we 'shouldn't' desire someone who loves and appreciates us and so on. Of course we will. That is what life is all about - knowing what we don't want so that we can create what we do want. But our happiness and other feel-good emotions do not have to depend on it. They come only from within and when we have discovered that they are not conditional on anything else, *that* is when wonderful things can start to happen.

Changing our thoughts and feelings isn't always a quick or easy process. And we are always likely to come up against resistance from other people who do not want us to change. They may feel threatened by our new way of looking at life, uncomfortable with it because, according to what they believe, it just isn't 'right', or maybe a little hostile because we are nudging awake some deep buried knowledge they are trying to ignore. In addition, our beliefs and thought patterns have become well-entrenched. But like any other habit, with steady practice and commitment we can do it. Think of a river bed and how over the years, the water has carved out a channel in the earth that the stream always follows. That river bed is like our habitual thoughts, carving out their own deep channel. But if we divert the river, setting it on a new path, eventually that new path will become as deep if not deeper than the original and that old, no longer wanted river bed will no longer be active. So too with our thoughts. Before long, our new, consciously chosen thoughts become our truths and our reality.

What this means
So, we are all 100% responsible for our thoughts, beliefs, feelings, actions and reactions. *Plus* for everything that 'happens' to us. No-one and no thing can impact on us unless we allow or attract it. Accepting this responsibility is scary (but so very exciting). We

don't like thinking that we have attracted something unwelcome in our lives. But *all* of life, the 'good' bits and the 'bad' bits, is our creation. And when you see everything that we have produced, it's mind-blowing. That's what life is all about!

The problem we have is that most of us create by default. We don't understand that we even have this power, let alone know how to use it, so we create our experiences unconsciously. And like everything we do without really thinking about it – and also because we tend to vibrate for much of the time at a level that cannot attract to us the things we really desire – these creations often end up being somewhat less than perfect. Our creations depend on our moods. But when we are living on emotional auto-pilot, our moods are governed by our creations. So, when life is good, it keeps on being good, or gets better. But when something happens that we allow to change our mood (in other words, our vibrations), the downward spiral begins. Once we begin to understand that it is all under our control, that we can choose to feel or think differently, then we become *conscious creators* and our lives are transformed. We no longer play the victim game, or the martyr game. We cannot, since we know that we alone are 100% responsible for what we are experiencing and can choose to change it.

Ditching the victim mentality
Don't people just love the victim thing? Switch on to any soap or news bulletin, look at any newspaper front page and chances are that there will be plenty of stories pushing the 'isn't life awful' or the 'poor me, aren't I hard done by' mentalities. Sadly, victimhood seems to be becoming an epidemic in our society today as many people become less and less willing to accept responsibility for anything. When occasionally someone refuses to play the game, to accept the victim label, to succumb to the low energies of the pervasive (and persuasive!) 'poor me' syndrome, my heart lifts.

On the back of this rising tide of victimhood the 'compensation culture' is growing. Someone else has to be found to blame and financially punished for the unwelcome things we experience, whether through *accident* or *error*. I have italicised these latter words as, once we assume full responsibility for our creations, we can see that these concepts do not and cannot exist. Once we know that we are solely responsible for everything that 'happens to' us, that there is no such thing as an *accident*, just an experience that we have for some reason attracted, they make no sense. Now I am not advocating that, with our current consciousness, it is in our highest and best interests for irresponsible and criminal actions to go unchallenged. Humankind, as a whole, does not yet have the necessary awareness to allow this. Rather like a young child who is prevented by a fireguard from touching the flames or held on a walking rein to stop her running out into the traffic, so we need to be compassionately protected until we have the necessary knowledge and wisdom to protect ourselves.

Then there is martyrdom. I'm sure every one of us knows at least one habitual martyr – there are a lot of them about. These are the people who like to be seen as 'brave', indispensable and self-sacrificing, who put up with things, usually with that familiar deep, heavy sigh. Who refuse help because they can manage – or rather want to have to manage and to let everyone else know what a burden it is but not to worry because they are fine.....

Victimhood and martyrdom are two sides of the same coin. Both are self-perpetuating. The more we give away our power, leaving ourselves feeling disempowered, helpless and victimised, the more we attract experiences into our lives that reinforce those feelings until they become our deep-seated truth. And in many ways, being a victim is easier. It often feels so much simpler and more comfortable to blame someone or something else, rather than to stand up, accept responsibility and act. But when you do, boy does it feel good! Most of us slide into these mindsets occasionally, even if it's just a 'Grrrr! Why are the traffic lights always on red when I'm tired and want to get home quickly?' And it feels horrible. As soon as we can shake ourselves out of it, we suddenly feel stronger, empowered, in control. Because we are!

A bit more on being a victim
If no-one is ever a victim, what about the hundreds of thousands who die of famine in Africa, or suffer the atrocities of war? What about children subjected to sexual and other horrific forms of abuse? Or those on the receiving end of natural disasters such as floods or earthquakes? Aren't they genuinely victims of circumstances beyond their control? This is a difficult question and one I have been trying to resolve for my own peace of mind for quite a while now. I have come up with the following thoughts.

• The Law of Attraction is objective, non-judgemental and unchanging. It doesn't see right or wrong, good or bad. It simply reacts to the vibrations we are giving off and brings us experiences that resonate with them. These may not be experiences we would choose to have.

• Group consciousness is a powerful magnet. If one person can attract something through their thoughts and fears, imagine how much more powerful it gets when a group of people is sending out the same vibration. My belief is that only those resonating in some way with that frequency will actually get caught up in the event. Anyone else either 'happens' to be somewhere else or has a 'lucky' escape.

• Current perception sees anyone who dies as being a victim. Our mindset is that death is the end and to be feared. Once we know that death is not an ending but just another step on our journey of adventure and a coming home to our True Self, it takes on a different light. As we are eternal, we can never 'die'. Our Soul can never cease to exist. We merely change form. Those we leave behind mourn their loss knowing that we have merely moved on rather than just ceased to be. This moving on is simply another Soul choice in our big adventure.

• Children are, in my belief, a slightly different issue and need to be considered a little differently. Although on a Soul level they are whole and fully developed, they are still getting used to being on the physical plane and in a human body. Both physically and emotionally, they are deeply dependent on other people for their wellbeing – and their survival. While the Law of Attraction governs them, as it does all of us, the newness of their experience allows them to be influenced and affected by the energies of those around them, particularly their parents and carers (and also by the beliefs and attitudes of the mother whilst they are still in the womb).

POWER THOUGHT
When you give away your power, you give away your dreams

Conscious Creation - another benefit

As we now know, because of the Law of Attraction, we are all in control of our own destiny. We write the storyline of our lives. If our reality is not how we wish it, once we accept and understand this we can deliberately and with awareness begin the process of manifesting what we do want. This is conscious creation.

If you have ever read or watched the DVD of *The Secret*[4] or read *Cosmic Ordering*[5] you may believe that the Law of Attraction is just a huge virtual superstore that is waiting to deliver to you all the material goodies you have ever dreamed of: wealth, a sports car, a beautiful home by the sea... And yes, it will do that and there is nothing wrong with wanting any or all of them. We are physical beings in a physical world and those things are part and parcel of enhancing our experience and enjoyment of it. But it is also so much more than that. Through its processes we create the whole fabric of our lives. Not just the big one-offs like your soul-mate, a successful career or that Porsche but also the general and constant flow of our everyday existence. It dictates whether our lives are easy, smooth and flowing, or filled with set-backs and obstacles. We can choose to bring in such qualities as inner peace and harmony, good health, fulfilment, love, joy or wisdom - those essential blessings that money can't buy and which, at the end of the day, are all that we are really looking for. Whatever you dream of, the process is exactly the same.

Learning the art of conscious creation
We can only attract into our lives those things that match the energy vibrations we are giving out. As an analogy, in the UK if you tune your radio to 88-91fm you will pick up BBC Radio 2. You will not pick up Radio 4. Another way I like to look at it is to see myself as a giant electro-magnet that is always switched on. My thoughts and feelings are the electro-magnetic power that inexorably pulls towards me everything that matches the frequency of its pulses.

In order then to manifest something specific in our lives we need to make sure our beliefs, feelings and thoughts are in harmony with it. To go back to our radio station analogy, if we wish to attract greater prosperity into our lives (Radio 4) but our predominant thoughts are tuned into all the bills we have to pay, our overdrafts or dwindling pension funds (Radio 2), Radio 2 is what we will get.

The reality that you are currently living is the sum of your beliefs and of all you have previously thought, felt and done. If it a place you are enjoying, great. If not, it isn't a problem as you can begin to change it - right in this moment - by choosing new thoughts and feelings that harmonise with your desires and make you feel better. If you can keep hold of these new thoughts and feelings more than you fall back into the old ones then you will see a gradual and continual unfolding of events that will, sooner or later, lead you to where you want to be.

POWER THOUGHT

You don't have to make it happen. You just have to allow it to happen

---

There are three steps to consciously creating our reality. We only have to think about the first and third steps. Source takes care of the second. These steps are 1) Ask; 2) Be answered and 3) Allow yourself to receive.

Step 1. Ask. This is the easy bit. We are doing it all the time. Every thought and feeling that we send out is a vibrationary request that brings an immediate response (step 2). When we are consciously doing this however, there are some points to note that make our asking more effective:

- focus on what you want, not what you don't want. Obvious? Maybe, but it's where a lot of people fall down because they are focussing their attention on the current 'What Is' rather than their desired outcome. The Law of Attraction cannot process negatives, so it will always register 'not want' as 'want'. If you desire more money, for example, keep your thoughts on your future prosperous lifestyle and away from a current reality of debts and perceived lack.
- have complete and total faith that your request has been heard and granted (it has!). Know without a shadow of a doubt it is yours, give thanks and let go both of your request and of any attachment to the outcome.

Step 2. Be answered. Source, through the Law of Attraction, always says Yes, unequivocally. Our requests are not vetted or censored – every one gets a Yes response. In other words, 'Be careful of what you ask for, you just might get it.'

Step 3. Allow yourself to receive. This is much harder. We can all ask and we all do - all the time. But not so many of us are able to allow ourselves to receive our desires. Allowing means, primarily, keeping our energy frequencies in steady and constant harmony with our desires, getting out of our own way and believing we deserve what we are asking for.

If you don't see any sign of your desire manifesting, above all – BE PATIENT. Everything happens in divine perfect timing. This may not be as quickly as you would like. Maybe, for example, your ideal new partner isn't yet single or is living in a different country at present. Perhaps your perfect job doesn't yet exist, or your dream home is not yet available for you to move into. The latter happened recently to a friend of mine. Her house had been on the market for over two years, When she eventually agreed its sale, within a week she had found and signed the lease on a beautiful country cottage that ticked virtually every box on her wish list – a cottage that had only become vacant a month previously.

However, there are a few things you can check to ensure you aren't getting in your own way:

- Do you really want what you have asked for? Has the request come from your heart or from your head? Is it something you feel you 'should' want or that someone else thinks is right for you, or is it a genuine passionate desire?
- Is your focus on the 'want' or on the 'don't want'? Remember, the Law of Attraction responds to the target of your thoughts and feelings, not to the 'wants' or 'don't

wants' that go along with it.

- Do your vibrations match your desire? Are you feeling upbeat, excited and certain? Or do you doubt it will manifest, maybe worry about what might happen if it does? Are you feeling generally good, happy and positive? (This will always boost your creative power.)
- Do you believe that it is possible for you to have it and that you deserve it?
- Can you feel the feeling of having it? Visualise (daydream) about having it in your life – how you will feel, how you will live. But restrict your daydreaming to the end result only, don't start imagining how it will come about.
- Have you let go of all need, desperation, impatience and expectation? If not, do so and then get on with your life. Let it come to you when the time is right.
- Are you listening to your inner guidance? Often we need to take action to manifest our dreams but if we aren't listening to our guidance, we may be taking the wrong action, or acting when we should be sitting back and waiting. Above all, we must not try to 'make it happen', which will push everything away. Instead, listen to your intuition and follow its nudges. A caution: if you are ever guided to do something that feels uncomfortable, life squashing or just plain wrong, leave it alone. It will be Ego getting in on the act. True inner guidance will always be loving, positive and life-affirming.
- Are you trying to work out how it will come about? That is not your job. Let the 'how-to's take care of themselves. That is the task of Source. The Law of Attraction is limitless, because the creative energy of Source is limitless. There is no end to the intricate, miraculous and even magical ways our dreams can become our reality. But our thought processes can only work within the limited framework of our conscious mind. Source has no such restrictions and

sees and understands the whole picture. Because of this, Source can create perfect solutions that are beyond our wildest imaginings.

If you have ticked all the above boxes and still nothing is showing up, it is helpful to investigate your subconscious beliefs, which will sabotage any attempt to attract something into your life if they are in conflict with it. Do you spend, spend, spend every time you have a bit of spare cash? Do you always walk away from relationships before they have a chance to turn into something meaningful? Do you work all hours yet success, recognition or a salary increase is never forthcoming? All these scenarios and many, many more are the results of our subconscious beliefs sabotaging us. If we have a long-held and deep desire for something in our lives that we don't yet have, a desire that comes from the heart rather than our head, it is very likely that a subconscious belief (maybe more than one) is blocking it. Once we uncover and release these beliefs, the floodgates open.

It is often more helpful to work with a therapist or able and trusted friend when we are digging to uncover these beliefs. When we go solo Ego, in the mistaken belief that it is protecting us, very often blocks us from getting to where we need to be. An objective persistent ally can help us get round these ego blockades. I have personally found EFT (Emotional Freedom Technique)[6] to be extremely effective but many other processes, including hypnotherapy, can be equally helpful.

POWER THOUGHT

Expect without expectation – source unknown

A thought

Of course, if no-one and nothing outside ourselves creates our experiences, then we cannot and do not create anyone else's, whether that is their feelings, their thoughts, their beliefs or their situations. Only they can do that. Everything that is going on in their lives, they have attracted. We are not, and can never be, responsible for anyone else's happiness (or misery) regardless of what they would have us think.

But doesn't that give us carte blanche to behave as callously, cruelly or thoughtlessly as we like? Well, in some ways yes, but if we do so, we will only affect those people who are vibrationally matched to allow such actions into their lives, or who are attracting it through their beliefs and fears (This is not a licence to behave in this way, which is totally contrary to who we really are). Another important thing to remember is that what we ourselves experience depends on the vibrations we are sending out. So if we are acting on a lower level vibration of callousness, unkindness and the like, we will be attracting exactly those frequencies back into our own lives. Do we really want to do that?

If we try our best to act always as our Soul would act, we will always come from a place of love, trust and knowledge that our actions will always be for the highest good of everyone concerned. And that we will be attracting like experiences into our reality. How that impacts on other people is up to them.

That's all there is to it. But of course, it isn't necessarily quite as easy as it sounds. Our thoughts and emotions constantly carve out their own channels, called neural pathways, within us. The longer we've held them and the more we revisit them the more established these pathways become. Changing them requires a real desire and commitment to do so, but it can be done.

Taking responsibility is one of the most powerful tools of transformation we can use. Start now and watch as life expands.

> **POWER THOUGHT**
> All that we are is the result of what we have thought -
> Buddha

Key 2

Leave fear behind

So... Life is this wonderful, exciting gift. It has been given to us for the sole purpose of joy, based on the freedom to be, do and have anything we desire. Life is to be grasped blissfully, gratefully, enthusiastically; lived to the full, experienced in all its wonderful variety. It is a magical journey of love, happiness and discovery.

Great stuff! But if that is the case, why then do we rarely experience it like this? Why, for so many of us, is life a struggle, stressful, something to be got through despite a lack of money, unsatisfying relationships and work, less than perfect health or any other obstacle to this paradise we are promised? Because we have forgotten it. Because, while we come into our physical bodies knowing only love, remembering that love is all that is really real, we soon forget it all. Little by little, we learn fear – from our parents, our teachers, our religious leaders, our cultures. All of whom have, in their turn, learnt fear from their parents, their teachers, their religious leaders and their cultures and so on back through the generations. We forget that we are all One and we begin to live in separateness – which only increases our fear.

What fear does

Fear squashes us into a box and throws away the key. Fear limits us, suffocates us and disempowers us. It prevents us reaching out for our dreams and achieving all that we are capable of achieving. Fear stops us being truly alive.

Fear is what we experience when we do not feel in the driving seat, when we believe ourselves to be at the mercy of factors outside ourselves, whether other people, nature, fate, the economic climate or anything else. We believe we have very little, if any, control over these things. That causes us feelings of helplessness and powerlessness and, as a result, fear. However, as we have seen, since we are the creators of everything we experience, nothing can just 'happen to' us. We create or allow it all. Once we really truly *know* this, we can learn to take charge of what we experience, and to see it from a different perspective – because it all comes from within ourselves. Then we can begin to release our fear and to move to a life lived through love. Love sets us free, in the truest sense of the word. Free to be all that we can be. It opens our hearts and minds and allows us to reach for our deepest dreams and desires, without limit or condition.

Fundamentally, love and fear are the only two emotions that exist. They sit at the root of everything, including every other emotion we feel. Our every action, our every thought, depends on whether we are coming from a place of love or a place of fear. All of the positive, feel-good emotions – joy, enthusiasm, compassion, excitement – are born of love. Every negative, feel-bad emotion – criticism, guilt, resentment, depression, lack of self-worth – is born of fear. The way we feel colours everything else we do – what we say, what we think, how we act... And what we experience.

Yet, when we look closer still, we see that all that really exists is love. Fear is not a 'thing'. It is the absence of a thing. In the same way that dark is merely the absence of light, so fear is the absence of love. Therefore, when true unconditional love exists, fear cannot. By learning to live in love, we banish fear.

Why we invented fear
When the first souls entered physical form, we did not know fear. It hadn't been 'invented' yet. We lived in joy, peace and abundance. But in order to truly know something, to fully experience it, we have to have something to measure it against.

We have to know its opposite, what it is not. So, to truly know, experience and appreciate joy, love and peace, we also have to know and experience what love, joy and peace are not. And what joy, love and peace are not, is fear and the emotions and actions it gives birth to. So we invented fear. However at that time we still remembered that fear is just an illusion and that love is all that is really real, so we were not governed by it.

As we became more and more involved in our physical existence with all its unique experiences, as we moved away from our hearts and into our heads, we gradually forgot who we were, where we had come from and all that we knew. We began to believe that this flesh and blood life was all there is and fear became dominant. If we believe death to be the end, anything that threatens life, whether real or imagined, creates fear. We forgot the supremacy of love and the tool became the master.

Almost everything we said or did was governed by fear – fear of the dark, fear of vengeful gods, fear of weakness, fear of anything different or unknown. As we developed and became more 'civilised', our fears also developed and evolved. Rulers and religions controlled their subjects through fear, themselves fearful of losing their power and status. Fear of hunger, poverty, disease, death or losing a loved one afflicted everyone (and still does). The very few who still lived solely in love, remembering their True Self and knowing that fear is merely illusion, were either classed as lunatics, heretics or – very occasionally – holy. And very often they were considered to be too dangerous by those who ruled as they threatened their power and control and so, in many cases, they were 'made examples of'.

Has anything changed today? Very little. We may be afraid of different things, but the people of this beautiful planet Earth are still ruled by fear. Big business, governments and religions need it. It's what keeps them powerful and influential. And fear engenders more fear. The Law of Attraction says that it must. So the world is becoming ever more fearful. Global communication, the internet, almost instantaneous coverage of man-made or natural disasters, war and every other unpleasant occurrence means we are bombarded constantly with images and messages that instil fear and its related emotions. TV programmes, films and computer games are becoming increasingly violent and frightening, mirroring the fears (and corresponding low vibrations) of society as a whole. Fear is, and always has been, firmly at the root of all perceived 'bad' behaviour, on every scale. It is well documented that a bully acts the way he/she does through a sense of deep insecurity. The same can be said for war or religious intolerance.

As I'm writing this chapter, the world is in the middle of massive financial upheaval. Every day the papers and news programmes are full of misery with 'experts' telling us how bad it is and how much worse it's going to get (usually with an almost perverse glee and desire to be proven right). Unfortunately this creates a self-fulfilling prophecy. It spreads an ever-growing fear. People (even those with plenty of money) are afraid to spend it, further depressing the economy and exacerbating the situation. Once again, fear is creating the very situation that people fear.

Happily, not all is gloom and doom. Now is also the time of a huge shift in consciousness within humankind. Many people are waking up to a new possibility – the possibility of choosing to live in love, joy and co-operation rather than fear. In doing so, they are inspiring others to explore the thoughts they are offering. By raising their own frequency, they are contributing to raising the vibration of all of humanity.

POWER THOUGHT

It is our choice whether we step forward in love and joy
... or hold ourselves back in fear, scarcity & limitation

Let it go

Easier said than done? Yes, of course it is. We have been programmed from birth to be fearful. Sometimes, when we were young, our parents' cautions were wise and helpful: *'Don't touch the oven. It's hot.'* Or: *'Don't run across the road without looking'*. But as we grow, many of these fears become outdated. Cautions that served us well as children may now limit us as adults. But how many more were totally irrelevant, based on their own learned fearful beliefs? Fears that family or friends or society want us to hang onto so that we don't rock the boat? Fears that, because of the Law of Attraction, frequently become self-fulfilling prophesies? Maybe you recognise some of these fear-filled beliefs that many of us hold, but that don't serve us at all.

- *'If you show people how you really feel, no-one will like you.'* – fear of being authentic, of being ourselves. Fear of being alone, disliked or rejected. Feeling we aren't good enough as we are.
- *'You can't go out looking like that! What will people say?'* – fear of standing out, of being different, of being noticed. Fear of ridicule, of other peoples' judgement.
- *'Never trust a man/woman'.* – fear of relationships, of the opposite sex. Fear of trusting anyone, of allowing ourselves to be vulnerable. Fear of being hurt.
- *'I'm going to fit a burglar alarm. You hear about so much crime these days!'* – if we worry excessively about being burgled, guess what we'll attract!
- *'I don't drive on motorways. They are too dangerous.',* - the same applies.

And so on and so on. I'm sure you can list plenty more examples of your own that you have heard from well-meaning sources.

Many of our fears hide in our subconscious and we don't even know we have them. They are often irrational, even ridiculous, but they are there. They are insidious, lurking invisibly, only becoming apparent when we seek the reasons why we continually sabotage the fulfilment of our desires. Our subconscious mind is the huge submerged base of the iceberg, our conscious mind only the tip. So whatever we think we believe in our conscious mind is irrelevant if our subconscious fears contradict it. These fears may have been drummed into us over a period of time, but also may have come from one minor incident while we were growing up, or from misreading some information we were given. That makes them no less powerful. If there is an area of your life that is not working, you can bet there are some fears, conscious or subconscious, skulking behind it.

The sad fact is that most of our fears are unjustified and simply 'wrong', in the sense that they are untrue and do not serve us. But, as the Law of Attraction always brings us what we put our attention on and have strong emotions about – and as fear is an incredibly powerful emotion – the more fearful we are, the more reasons to be fearful we attract into our lives. Depending on the depth of our fears and how much we focus on them, this can be as 'harmless' as noticing newspaper headlines, hearing news stories or conversations (although actually, as it feeds our fears further, it isn't harmless at all), to creating in our own lives the actual experiences we are afraid of.

Happily however, once we start living more in love and refusing to give time or attention to fear, we begin to attract more love and positive energy into our lives. When we deny fear its power over us, so the things we once feared no longer affect us – or if they do, we can see the positive 'silver linings' they bring. Living in love, dispelling our fears, allows us to live life to the full, to reach our full potential without sabotaging ourselves on the way, to be open and joyfully accepting of all the wonderful experiences life offers us.

How many times have you really wanted to do something but haven't because:

a) my husband/wife/best friend/parents (you can put in anyone that applies here) wouldn't like it if I did.

b) what would people say?

c) I could look a right idiot if it all goes wrong.

d) it's too risky. I might fail.

And so on and so on and so on......

SO WHAT? If you want to do (or have, or be) something so much it aches, and if it feels so-o-o-o 'right' to do/have/be it, go ahead. If it all goes pear-shaped, again so what? At least you've tried – and you won't spend the rest of your life sitting wondering 'What if?'. There are few thoughts sadder than 'What if?'. However if you are following your true desires and you are approaching them always from love, knowing that you deserve to fulfil them and that everything is working out perfectly, Source has a marvellous way of going about things that creates wonderful win-win situations for everyone concerned. What is more, because Source always says Yes to those desires, you will find all sorts of opportunities that will lead you to their fulfilment appearing before you.

Life is all about living, and living is all about experiencing. All the reasons for not doing something you long to do are always based in fear. And this includes not doing that something because of the impact on those you love. Do yourself a huge favour, and from now on base all your decisions on love.

POWER THOUGHT

'Too many of us are not living our dreams because we are living our fears' - Les Brown

---

I have turned down many wonderful opportunities in my life, from parties to a chance to work in Paris. Things I would have loved to have done but said 'No' to. Why? Because I was afraid. Afraid of going it alone, of stepping out of my comfort zone. Afraid of what other people might think. Afraid of hurting someone close to me. Afraid mostly though of leaving the safe and familiar, if unfulfilling and life-squashing, behind and stepping into the unknown without a safety net. Oh, I had plenty of really good reasons for not doing this or that at the time, but the bottom line was that I was afraid to. And yet, on the occasions when I took a chance, it all worked out and also, I grew.

It is only recently, as my understanding has increased, that I have seen and recognised the patterns of my life. Always there were good excuses – and always they were a cover up for my fears. Beliefs instilled in me from childhood that the world wasn't a friendly place to be and that I should play it safe. I am still working on clearing these issues and progress is sometimes very slow. But now that I see why I act the way I do it is easier to change. This book is a good example. I have wanted to write a book and have it published for a very long time. Since I was a child. And yet I never really tried. Perhaps a few rough scribbles here and there but nothing serious. Why? Because I was afraid – afraid I wasn't good enough, afraid I would fail. It didn't occur to me that if I loved to write, it didn't matter – and that there was no basis at all for my fears.

So, how do you know whether you are coming from love or fear? Well, just ask yourself two easy questions:

1) Does the thought of doing/saying/having it make me feel good or bad?
2) Is doing/saying/having it life-enhancing or life-squashing? When something feels good and life-enhancing, it is coming from a place of love. Uncomfortable, life-squashing feelings are always based in fear.

You can ask the same questions with your thoughts. If a thought feels heavy, restricting, disempowering, it is a thought coming from fear. If it feels good, light and expanding, then you can be sure that it is love speaking to you. As a bonus, every time we are in 'love mode' our vibrations rise. And as our vibrations rise, good and then better things flow to us. On the other hand, fear lowers our vibrations and we attract less good, less wanted experiences. So it really is a bit of a no contest! In this, as in everything in life, we _always_ have a choice. We can choose to hold ourselves back in fear, scarcity and limitation – or we can choose to step forward in joy, love and trust.

Not long ago, I chanced across a healing course that I immediately knew was right for me. And I hesitated to book it. I kept going back to it and, after dithering for a couple of hours, I finally sat down and asked myself if the reason I didn't just go ahead and book it was fear. The answer was a very clear 'Yes'. My bank account was more or less empty and at the time I had just about enough money coming in to cover my bills, but _not_ to pay £500.00 for a course and accommodation. I was afraid I wouldn't have enough money. I was also facing my longstanding fear of stepping out of my comfort zone. I had slipped into fear and into lack. As soon as I realised that, I booked my place immediately. I had recognised and released the fear that was holding me back.

The course was superb and exactly what I had been looking for, and it gave me an avenue to start increasing my income as well as a tool that would accelerate my spiritual growth. I also discovered that somehow, despite the financial outlay I still had the money I needed. Now I am not recommending you go mad and recklessly splash cash you don't have willy-nilly, (getting ourselves into debt is not a great way to raise our vibrations!) but if there is something you are strongly drawn to do and it feels so right, then bite the bullet and do it. The money _will_ come if you are in the right place.

Remember, we are all sparks of divinity, fragments of Source energy. As such, we (as our True Self) know only pure, unconditional love. We know that fear is just an illusion. The more we can reconnect with that higher, remembering bit of ourselves, the easier it is for us to release fear and live in love. In the next chapter, we will look at more ways of putting this into practice.

POWER THOUGHT

Unsquash your life

Key 3

Choose love

Our Soul, our True Self, lives only and always in a state of unconditional love. In that place, we know no fear, no pain nor any other negative life-squashing emotion. We understand that everyone, everything, every situation is absolutely OK, just as it is. We know that everyone is behaving in the exactly the 'right' way for them to behave, based on their current understandings and life experiences to date. We see the divine, the spark of Source in everyone (including ourselves!) and we know the connection between us. And we know that the Universe is a truly loving and supportive place. We stop the 'shoulds', the 'oughts' and the 'buts'. We stop finding fault and instead find the joyful and beautiful. (Finding fault always destroys our own inner peace and joy since it creates such a chasm between what we are feeling and our True Self.)

When we live in love, we are healthier, happier and more abundant, because we are able to allow all the gifts of Source to flow to us without hindrance. We experience life and the world around us in a totally new way. There are many people, I am aware, who will say that this is simply looking at the world through rose-tinted spectacles and denying reality. But reality is what we choose it to be, not how someone else sees it, and if we see life, the world and the people in it as a loving and joyful, and ourselves as deserving to be loved in return, then that will be our reality. When we live in true, unconditional love, we see the beauty and divinity in everything around us, even when it is hidden and hard to find.

Living in love has other benefits too. Our relationships, careers, prosperity and dreams are richer and more fulfilling. Life flows smoothly and effortlessly. Plus, we live longer, healthier and more satisfying lives. One of my must-read books is *The Biology of Belief* by Bruce Lipton[1], an eminent US cellular biologist. In his book he teaches us how all our body's cells have two modes – growth and protection. In growth mode, everything is working to its optimum, our cells are vital and active, growing and replacing themselves and, very importantly, releasing energy into our bodies. In protection mode, our cells effectively close down and become dormant. Protection mode is regulated by, principally, the adrenal glands. This function evolved originally as a survival mechanism, allowing us to flee from sabre toothed tigers and other such dangers – the fight or flight mechanism. As Bruce Lipton explains, when faced with a life-threatening situation, all our physical resources need to be focussed on escaping that danger and surviving. Anything that doesn't contribute to that function closes down.

Unfortunately, although our minds can tell the difference between a sabre-toothed tiger and a bad day at the office, our bodies can't. So they react to stress, anger, judgement and all our other fear-based emotions (all of which release adrenalin into our body) in the same way, shutting down their creative growth mechanisms. But Bruce Lipton takes it one step further than this, writing *'It is also important to note that to fully experience your vitality it takes more than just getting rid of life's stressors. In a growth/protection continuum, eliminating the stressors only puts you at the neutral point in the range. To fully thrive, we must not only eliminate the stressors but also actively seek joyful, loving, fulfilling lives that stimulate growth processes.'* In other words, if we want to enjoy the best health we are capable of experiencing, we must deliberately, consciously and continually choose to live our lives in ways that that brings us joy, love and satisfaction.

POWER THOUGHT

In the eyes of Source, all is perfect, healed and whole. All
dis-ease, dis-comfort and dis-harmony are merely
illusion. I now choose to look past the illusion and to see
the perfection beyond.

Learn to live in love

Practise non-judgement

When we judge, whether other situations, other people or
ourselves, we are coming from fear. We judge things as being
either right or wrong, good or bad, acceptable or unacceptable,
perfect or faulty. But our Higher Self does not see life in this way.
From its place of love, it sees no good or bad, right or wrong, only
what is. And what is, just – is. Good and bad, right and wrong are
judgements we make based on the lessons we have learned and
the beliefs and fears we have absorbed. These judgements are
always personal and subjective. They cannot be anything else.
Even when there is a so-called consensus of opinion and 'society'
agrees on what to label good and acceptable and what not, these
judgements always change. Take smoking for example. Only fifty
or so years ago, smoking was considered a must-do. It was 'cool'
and sophisticated. Contrast that to the general attitude of our
society towards cigarettes today. Or women's rights. Or slavery.
Attitudes and perceptions change and it is these attitudes and
perceptions that create our judgements of good and bad. It could
be argued that as we learn and evolve we 'see the error of our
ways'. So, assuming that, what we know without a doubt to be
wrong and bad today could well be good and right tomorrow
(and vice versa!).

Judging makes us feel self-righteous, better than.
Unfortunately this is a low energy feeling. And our energy falls
even further as we gripe and complain and gossip and bitch

about whatever it is we are being judgemental of. Even seemingly small things, like commenting critically on someone's appearance, speech or mannerisms, is insidious and harmful to our wellbeing. It may make us feel a little better in the short term, but only at the expense of making someone or something else wrong or 'less than'. It lowers our vibrations and attracts to us experiences that match that lower plane. These may well not be experiences we would want or enjoy. And it is a hollow victory, based on our own fear of not being good enough. When we know we are good enough as we are, we don't have to prove it by comparing ourselves to others, which is exactly what happens when we judge.

I feel it is important though to distinguish between judgement and preference. We can dislike something without seeing it as bad or wrong. For example, I dislike bananas intensely. I find even the smell extremely unpleasant. But should I judge bananas as 'bad' or 'wrong' just because I don't like them? Of course not. Likewise there are people whose company I enjoy and those who I prefer not to spend time with. This is my personal preference. It doesn't mean these are 'bad' or 'wrong' people and there will be many others who do enjoy their company.

When we learn to be non-judgmental, we see the good in everyone, including ourselves. And let's face it, no-one is ever harder on us than we are on ourselves. We are our harshest critic, our most severe judge, our fiercest opponent. We constantly beat ourselves up about what we 'should' or 'shouldn't' have done, said or thought. Why? Because the majority of us grow up with the message that we aren't good enough as we are.

Practise first of all non-judgment and unconditional love on yourself. Once you have mastered not judging and unconditionally loving yourself, it is much easier to do it with others. Instead of seeing things as good or bad, right or wrong, we learn to just see them 'as', even when we desire something else. We don't necessarily have to like or enjoy every experience but we can know that each one, even those we would prefer not to have, brings us a gift and an opportunity to grow. Non-judgement means allowing everything to be as it is, even when it is not how you would prefer it to be.

Not long ago, I had a wonderful lesson in living in love. I was spending a couple of days at a retreat centre when the owner asked for suggestions on how he could better have handled a sulky, disruptive teenager who has recently attended the retreat with his parents (clearly against his will). The answer came from a man from whom love, compassion and peace emanated from every pore – 'Just love him more.' The simplicity and truth of this statement almost knocked me sideways and reached deep into my heart. Instead of suggestions on how to control, change or 'fix' the young man, the answer was just to accept him how he is, and love him. Because if someone is behaving in a way that we find uncomfortable or challenging it is always based in fear, however well disguised or unrecognised. (And it is also always reflecting some aspect of ourselves that we are denying.) The best antidote for fear is love. The two cannot co-exist. When we are able to open our hearts and allow acceptance, love and compassion for all life to flow, then we are fully connected to our True Self.

Love What Is
What is...is! You are where you are in your life right now. Whether you are happy or unhappy there it makes no difference. In this moment you cannot be anywhere else. Railing against it, complaining, criticising, judging, getting angry – none of it does any good. None of it changes anything in this moment. It just makes us feel bad. And if we feel bad, the Law of Attraction resonates with those low energy vibrations – and eventually brings us more things to feel bad about.

In accepting and allowing What Is, we open to the opportunity to change it, to reach for something we would prefer.

Loving What Is doesn't mean we have to like it (loving and liking are two very different things). It doesn't mean we can't feel sad, or hurt, or any other emotion. It simply means not judging the situation as 'bad' or 'wrong'. It means allowing and feeling our emotions – and then letting them pass through us and move on. It means knowing, with a deep inner conviction, that even if we are really uncomfortable in the place where we are, everything is exactly as it needs to be in this moment.

Once you accept and allow, once you can love What Is, you are no longer pushing against something that you don't want. You are no longer resisting. And as what we resist, persists,[2] dissolving resistance is the most effective way of creating change.

A couple of years ago I became very upset when a very dear friend of mine, someone I was very close to, started seeing someone else. He had every right to – we weren't in any kind of relationship – but I felt a lot of emotional pain over it. After a couple of weeks of feeling extremely upset, then angry and throwing things around the house, and then upset again, and so on and so on, I realised that by acting the way I was, I was not helping the situation one bit. (I wasn't helping me either. With my vibrations at such a low level, I was blocking anything positive coming into my life - and attracting more negatives!). Things were as they were and nothing I could do would change that. So, even though I was finding the experience very painful, I decided to accept the situation. I immediately felt better – like I had stopped banging my head against the wall – and interest-ingly, within a week or so, the new relationship had begun to fizzle out. Coincidence...? Maybe. But by taking my 'not want' energy away from it, I was no longer giving it power in my life and thus attracting more of the 'not want' experience.

> ## POWER THOUGHT
> I accept and allow this current situation completely, even whilst desiring change, as I know that in fully accepting and allowing it, that which I do desire flows to me

In addition, when we come up against unwanted experiences, Source is bringing us the opportunity of contrast. Without contrast, without experiencing things we don't want, how do we know what we really do want? How can we know what 'hot' is if we have never experienced 'cold'? Contrast sharpens our preferences and desires and the greater the gap between what we are experiencing and what we wish to experience, the more powerful the vibrationary magnetism – *provided* we focus on the desired situation and not the current one. For example, on a cold rainy evening you may have the opportunity of going out to a lovely old pub to spend some very pleasant time with some close friends. Alternatively, you could choose to snuggle up by the fire with a good book or film and a glass of wine. Both options sound good and you would be very happy with either. The contrast is not that great and therefore the desire for one over the other is not strong. Compare that with thoughts of sitting in a cosy pub, chatting and laughing if you are sleeping rough without warmth or shelter. Now the contrast is much wider and the desire for your preferred experience much more powerful. However, in these situations most of us are too intent on saying 'No' to What Is to focus on and say 'Yes' to what we would prefer. Remember, as far as the Law of Attraction and vibrationary matches are concerned, saying 'No' *is* saying 'Yes'!

It also brings up hidden issues that we may be unaware of but which are hindering our joyful and free-flowing journey through life. This is life acting as a mirror, reflecting our true beliefs and feelings back to us to be recognised and understood. The experience I described a little earlier concerning my friend certainly did all of this. I came to realise that, despite my often vocal claims (which I genuinely believed) about the joys of singledom, at that time I actually did want a special someone in my life. It also brought up a lot (and I mean a LOT!) of deeply buried fears and emotions for me to clear. Phew! What a gift. Actually what a truly great gift. As a result of the insights and releases I received, I can now see why I have repeatedly acted and felt as I have in the past and why I have attracted the experiences I have had. That understanding is allowing me to break the patterns of the past and to create a new reality.

Love and accept yourself
We are wonderful, miraculous, magical beings, created from a fragment of Source. Everything we will ever need is already within us and our potential is limitless. How much more do you want to be? You are already the perfect You. So why do so few of us know this? And even when we 'know' it, why do we find it so hard to accept?

Our love for ourselves, our belief in ourselves and in our ability to succeed is inherent in each one of us as babies, when we joyfully accept and delight in every part of ourselves, knowing we are perfect. But all too often this deep love and certainty gets crushed and trampled as we grow, through the fears we absorb and messages we receive, often through the well-meaning actions of those who care for us. We aren't clever enough, or pretty enough, or tall enough, or strong enough. We don't have the 'right' education, attitude or talents. We come from the 'wrong' background, or we are the 'wrong' sex or weight or colour. We are told that we should keep our feet on the ground and let go of our 'impossible' dreams. Or that we shouldn't go 'blowing our own trumpet'. Or 'who do you think you are to believe you could actually do THAT?' (whatever THAT happens to be). Or a thousand other insidious messages impressing on us that, basically, we just aren't good enough.

These messages come to us from a number of different sources. Whilst most are received and taken on board by us when we are children (it is widely accepted that the majority of our beliefs are instilled in us by the age of 7), others sneak into our subconscious throughout our lives. These sources may include:

- parents, grandparents & other family: the messages we receive from our parents and family, deliberately or unwittingly, are strongly anchored. We may just have unloving critical parents but more often than not they are just trying to help us in the best way they know how. However, as no-one can teach what they do not know, their attempts are limited to what they themselves have learned about life.
- our peers, classmates and friends.
- our school teachers, (especially primary school teachers) whose opinions have a huge impact on our self-belief and self-worth as we grow.
- society and the media: how many of us women have not at some point felt a 'less than' feeling, no matter how slight, at all those air-brushed, digitally-enhanced, perfect (and unreal!) bodies in magazines? Or because we find it almost impossible to hold down a job, run a home and be the perfect mother and partner all at once. Men don't get away with it either, being constantly bombarded with similar punishing messages regarding amongst other things, their looks, success, wealth or sexual prowess..
- our cultural background: it wasn't all that many years ago that women were widely seen as weaker, less capable and less intelligent than men, a belief that some women (and men!) still carry with them today.
- lovers: we always believe more easily those people with whom we have close emotional ties.

and

religion: when our religious leaders teach us that we are 'sinners' and need to seek redemption and forgiveness, when even our ever-loving God sees us as wanting, how can we believe differently?

Let's get one thing clear here. All the judgemental, negative and otherwise unhelpful messages we have ever received are INCORRECT. They have everything to do with the person giving them and nothing to do with us. It is that person's beliefs and opinions, reflecting their own issues and attitudes and subject to all the messages that they in turn have taken on board, absorbed from yet other peoples' messages and beliefs... and so on, back through time.

Do yourself a *HUGE* favour. Forget every limiting, unhelpful, life-squashing comment you have ever received. Each of us already possesses all the attributes we will ever need. Everything we need to succeed is already within us and we all have the ability to reach our dreams. If we didn't, Source wouldn't have given them to us.

You are perfect at being you. You don't need to be fixed or made right. You are the sum of all your life experiences, mingled with your Soul. Yes, there may be things that you wish to change or develop, but that doesn't make you bad, wrong or unworthy as you are. We can all grow and evolve if we choose to but that doesn't take away one bit from the fabulous-ness of who we are now. A baby grows, learns and evolves into a child, and then an adult; a caterpillar into a butterfly; a rose bud into a fully blown bloom; a tiny acorn into a huge oak tree. Does that make the baby any less perfect than the adult, or the acorn less than the tree? If you don't 'get it right', be kind and gentle to yourself, forgive yourself if you feel it is necessary and accept that it is OK. We all make mistakes. It's part of our growth process. Just as you would with a child who is learning to read, or ride a bike, be patient with yourself and know that, as you are always growing, you will always make mistakes. Without stretching ourselves and reaching for more, we cannot evolve and grow. 'Not getting it right' isn't getting it wrong, it's learning!

We find it *so* hard to see ourselves as perfect, just as we are. Maybe we don't want to, because being perfect feels such a high standard to live up to, or because we feel it is an arrogant or conceited thing to do. Or perhaps (more likely!) because it is so far removed from how we see ourselves. I was on a retreat a year or so ago where a light-hearted comment was made about one of the other guests 'trying to be perfect'. She immediately went on the defensive, repeatedly claiming that she had never said she was perfect, that she was far from it, etc, etc. This really shows to me how far we have come from our True Self, who knows without a shadow of doubt that we already *are* perfect, exactly as we are. And I'll happily admit to having to play with these issues myself. (I use the word 'play' because 'work' brings up echoes of struggling and efforting, which is an unhelpful activity and never gets us very far.) As I was mulling on this event later, I received the following affirmation, which for me, helps to bridge the conflict:

POWER THOUGHT
I am perfect in my imperfection

Not loving and appreciating ourselves enough is one of the major obstacles that stand in the way of us living the lives that we desire. It is important to understand that loving and appreciating ourselves fully doesn't mean that we go around believing ourselves better or more deserving than anyone else. Neither does it cause us to become arrogant, conceited or boastful. Those types of behaviour come from the Ego and are usually a cover for a strong sense of fear and insecurity and a deep lack of real self-worth. The sort of self-love I'm talking about is instead a strong and unconditional self-love that comes from the heart, from a powerful respect for ourselves and a heartfelt appreciation for the wonderful creation that we are. From a deep intuitive knowing that, while we are no better than anyone else, we are equally as fabulous and deserving. From remembering our divinity. When we can remember and know, with that deep inner knowing, that we are divine beings, we cannot *not* love ourselves. Love is who we are. If you are struggling to get a handle on how that feels, imagine your best friend ever. Tune into the love you feel for that person, the respect, admiration and appreciation you have for them. Does that make them 'too big for their boots' or 'full of themselves'? No, of course not. He or she is just a great person. That is the love to hold for yourself. Sadly, most of us don't feel even remotely this way, yet it is perhaps the greatest gift we can give ourselves.

Why it matters

When we are out of step with ourselves and who we truly are, when we see ourselves as 'not good enough', we block our wellbeing. If we don't believe we are worthy of love, even from ourselves, how can we allow good into our lives? We will not see ourselves as worthy and deserving of it. When we are self-critical and self-judging we are unable to see and appreciate (and therefore use and enjoy) our natural skills, talents and gifts. We impose limitations on ourselves and rarely reach for our dreams – because we don't believe we can succeed. We settle for second best (or less) in our lives because we don't believe we deserve more.

Lack of love for ourselves causes us to look elsewhere for love and approval, and yet we can never find it outside if it doesn't exist within us. So we become people pleasers, being good rather than happy. Perhaps we may start to take on the role of victim or martyr or rescuer. Or alternatively, we may believe we are past all hope and redemption, and our lives take an ever-faster downward spiral. We may self-abuse, neglecting our mind, body and emotions. Or we may seek comfort elsewhere, such as in addictions. Work, drink, food, shopping, sex, exercise and too many others to mention – all are ways of burying our desolation and lack of self-love.

On the other hand, when we can learn to love ourselves deeply and unconditionally we allow that wellbeing into our lives. We know we deserve all of it – the abundance, the joy, the health, the love. We know that we are capable of achieving anything we desire so we pursue our dreams with enthusiasm and excitement.

We accept ourselves *exactly* as we are (we know we are perfect in our perceived imperfection!) and welcome our Shadow sides as an important and integral part of our being. Our Shadows are the parts of us that we have repressed or denied because we have learned that they are unacceptable. If you grew up learning to be seen and not heard for example, your Shadow might be extremely vocal and boisterous. Our Shadow sides tend to pop up at the most inopportune moments. In the above case, it could be that you get drunk at a family gathering, 'disgracing' yourself, behaving totally 'out of character'. Our Shadows will not be repressed forever and denying them can result in powerful and unpleasant consequences, such as a usually quiet, repressed wife suddenly beginning a passionate and very public affair with a lecherous neighbour, or more horrifically, the abuse of children by celibate priests who have been forced to repress and deny their sexuality. Our Shadow sides are a part of us and we cannot deny and reject them without denying and rejecting chunks of ourselves – seeing part of our whole as unacceptable and 'bad'.

Once we learn to love ourselves fully, we are able to nurture and care for ourselves, accepting our Shadows and weaknesses, knowing our needs and happiness are of utmost importance. We are always authentic and true to ourselves, as we feel totally confident and safe in who we are, in our being-ness. And in feeling that love and appreciation for ourselves, we are better able to flow it to those around us, allowing us to care for others and for our world in a more effective and loving way.

12 steps to self-love

1. Clear out all the negative messages you have ever received that stand in the way of you knowing who and what you truly are – and of loving that person. Take a sheet of paper and write down all those that come to mind, without thinking about or analysing it too much. How many are life-squashing and unhelpful? Let them go. If you want, why not burn the piece of paper or flush it down the loo to symbolise releasing them completely?

2. Forgive yourself for perceived past mistakes or 'crimes' and release any guilt you feel about them. We all make mistakes. They are how we learn.

3. Let go of all unhelpful or abusive habits and relationships. You deserve better and as long as you are trapped in them you will find it hard to move forward.

(The above steps can be a lot easier said than done and if this is the case with you, it may help to work with a therapist you feel safe with. There are so many therapies you can choose from – just go with what feels right.)

4. Start appreciating yourself. Make a list of everything that is wonderful about you and bask in your glory. Only write those things you can genuinely believe. You can add to your list as you uncover more. (And you will, once you get in the flow)

5. Ask your friends and family the same question and **believe** them! (Pick carefully – you don't want *any*

negative comments.) Decide to believe their comments wholeheartedly, add them to your list.

6. Decide that from now on you are going to ignore every negative comment that is thrown at you. They stem from the other person's issues, not yours. Choose to focus only on the positive.

7. Louise Hay pioneered a technique known as Mirror Work, which involves standing in front of a mirror morning and night, looking yourself in the eyes and saying 'I love you.' This can be a really difficult exercise for many people but if you can persevere, the results are well worth it. If you really can't do it, Louise suggests beginning more gently by saying 'I am willing to love you.' Even 'You'll do!' is a helpful starting point (If you find yourself bursting into tears during this exercise, be gentle with yourself but do stick with it.)

8. Treat yourself as the wonderful precious being that you are, with love, care and gentleness. Release self-judgement and self-criticism. Allow yourself to make mistakes. Be nice to yourself. Surround yourself with things you love, whether people, objects or activities. Know that you deserve the best, just because you are alive.

9. Be your own best friend

10. Use affirmations – positive reinforcements of your new beliefs, such as 'I am loveable and loving', 'I am fabulous' or 'I deserve all the good the Universe can bring me'.

11. Accept and integrate your Shadow sides. By accepting our Shadows (not necessarily acting them out but allowing them to be) we accept and allow, and therefore are able to love, all of ourselves.

12. Be true to yourself.

We settle in life for what we believe we are worth. To have more or better, we have to know we deserve it. If we cannot fully love and appreciate ourselves, we can never believe we deserve it and therefore will not allow it into our lives.

POWER THOUGHT
Love is what is left when everything else is
stripped away

Be true to yourself

When we deeply love and appreciate ourselves, then we are able to show the world the authentic 'me'. Who we truly are. We drop all the masks and the acts and the pretence and we revel in being fully ourselves, speaking and acting from our truths. We do what is right and best for ourselves, putting our needs first and not being afraid to stand up for our wellbeing. We don't follow the herd when it doesn't fit comfortably with us.

This doesn't come easily to many of us. The lessons we learn growing up lead us to believe that we aren't good enough/likeable/loveable etc. We are so afraid that if we are ourselves no-one will want to know us. So, feeling that we aren't enough, we put on the masks and the characters and act out our lives the way we feel other people would like us to be. Or we believe we don't have the 'right' to be ourselves and that we have a duty or obligation to conform to how others want us to be. All of which stems from us not believing ourselves to be good enough or loveable enough or acceptable enough JUST AS WE ARE.

It takes so much energy to live inauthentically. When we are afraid to show our True Self for example, when we go out for the evening it may be that, consciously or unconsciously, we expend a huge and constant effort on making sure no-one sees through our deception. We can't fully let go and enjoy ourselves – it would be too risky, we might let the façade slip – and we are constantly thinking about what we should say and how we should say it, or how we should be acting/re-acting. An exaggeration? Absolutely not. I have known a number of people who feel and behave this way.

Alternatively, we may be afraid to go against the popular consensus and so find ourselves in situations we would rather not be in. This can be as serious as getting caught up in a criminal act – peer pressure, particularly amongst young people, makes it very difficult for someone to stand up for what he knows to be right for them – to as seemingly innocuous as going to watch a film you don't really want to see.

Perhaps the saddest aspect of trying to be someone we are not is that we lose sight of who we really are, of our dreams, even of our likes and dislikes as we try to fit in with the people around us.

POWER THOUGHT
To thine own Self be true

Key 4

Allow happiness in

Inextricably linked to living with love is living with joy. In fact, you cannot have one without the other. When we feel love, our hearts fill with joy. When we feel joy, our hearts burst with love: love for life, love for others, love for ourselves.

Following our hearts, doing the things that increase our happiness and joy, is the purpose of life. Through joy we create wonderful experiences that allow us to grow. We have already seen that life is not a trial to be endured, lessons to be learned, karma to be repaid, or any other form of struggle although most religions (and many 'New Age' philosophies as well) would have us believe that it is. Often it ends up that way – but that is because we make it so. Life is intended to be a glorious and joyful adventure, an exciting voyage of discovery.

Let it flow

Joy *is* Source. It is the free flow of Source energy into and through our experience. It is creation and it is love, flowing openly and without restriction through the essence of our being. It flows from Source and to Source in a constant cycle, replenishing and renewing itself constantly. It is Life. It is total and complete Wellbeing. It is Wisdom. It is always there, always flowing – it can never not be, for that is its nature.

Being happy raises our vibrations, which in turn are what attract everything – people, objects, events – into our lives. The happier, the more joyful we feel, the higher and lighter our vibrations. And the higher our vibrations, the more of all we desire, the more wonderful the people, experiences and things we attract into our lives.

So, in order to lead a fabulous life, to manifest easily and joyfully all our desires, we need to start following our hearts and living in happiness. As we have just seen, one big step forward in living a more joyful life is to live in a place of love. When we truly follow our hearts, we only ever do those things that make us feel on top of the world. Or enthral us so much we forget time. Or everything else around us. Following our hearts, doing what we love is so important in keeping us fit and healthy. Without joy in our lives, our physical body suffers and nothing flows. These magic moments are not a luxury. They are vitally important. Taking time out to recharge your batteries allows every area of your life to flow more easily. When I'm working, like everyone else I sometimes start to feel tense and stressed. Maybe I feel I have too much to do in too little time, or have a difficult problem to sort out. Or my computer crashes. The temptation is to slog on and catch up on my 'to do' list or battle with the problem – or throw something at the computer. None of which is productive or helpful. And whereas once that is exactly what I used to do, now I'll take time out and do one of the things on my 'Magic Moments' list instead. As I work from home, I'll often go for a walk around my 'estate' (a personal joke as I currently have a *very* small garden). It may be tiny but I love it and by the time I have looked at each plant, noticed the new buds and shoots and smelled the lavender, my energy has completely changed and I'm back in a good place from where I can start working more effectively again.

We so often feel that it is wrong to take this time out for ourselves, that we should just knuckle down and slog on with life. We consider it to be slacking or idling. Well even if it is, so what? To quote the famous poem 'Leisure' by W. H. Davies[1] :

WHAT is this life if, full of care,
We have no time to stand and stare?

My Grandma wrote this in my autograph book when I was a child and it has stayed with me ever since.

At a recent workshop I ran, I asked the people attending how many of them regularly took time off in their day to do something enjoyable just for themselves. Not one person raised a hand. I was a bit surprised to say the least, but perhaps I shouldn't have been. It is instilled in us from childhood that we have to work hard and keep our noses to the grindstone if we are to achieve anything at all. It's the mentality that 'life is a struggle' – and it's an extremely ineffective way of being. When we lighten up, life flows. Solutions, people and the things we need appear. We work more effectively and efficiently, getting more done in less time. Many enlightened businesses are now understanding this. They forbid their employees to work through their lunchtimes, knowing that they will be more productive for taking the break.

Why not create your own list of 'Magic Moments' – those things that take you out of the busy-ness of everyday life and into your Soul? On your list write down everything you love to do. Put down both the bigger, now-and-again things, such as 'holidaying on a desert island' and smaller things that you can fit into your everyday life. Perhaps you love to sit down with a coffee and a magazine, or a regular massage, or to chat to a friend on the phone. It is whatever makes *you* feel good. If you feel great bungee-jumping off a viaduct, go for it. It doesn't matter what anyone else says – it's *your* feel-good list. It's what works for you.

Here is a list of some everyday 'Magic Moments' that people have shared with me over the workshops I have led. If you are finding it hard to come up with enough of your own, why not use them for inspiration:

a hot bubbly bath by candlelight
gazing at the stars on a clear night

a hug (from a child, lover, friend or relative. It doesn't matter
   who)
baking cakes
making love
stroking a pet
dancing
skimming pebbles on the sea or a lake
sitting in a coffee shop, people watching
breathing in the scent of a rose
sunbathing (not politically correct I know, or good for the
   skin, but in small doses, boy does it make us feel good!)
running down a hill like you did when you were a child

I could be happy if..... I will be happy when..... But what
happens if and when those things come about? Usually we find
another excuse to put off our happiness, another reason why we
can't be happy now.

It's not always easy. People will ask,' How can I be happy
when....

- I've just lost my job
- I live in a really rough neighbourhood
- I find my work so unfulfilling

and so on, and so on....

You just need to decide to be, and then gradually move to new
thoughts and feelings that support your decision. Happiness,
success, wealth and anything else you desire are not dependent
on any external influence. These things come from within you
and depend solely on how you think, and as a consequence of
that, on how you feel. Where you live, how much money you
have, your state of health or anything else, none of it makes any
difference – unless you allow it to. And by changing your
thoughts about it, you send out more positive vibrations, which
in turn attract more positive solutions to those situations. As with
many of the processes in this book, it may not be easy – but it is

simple.

The simple truth is that being happy is a choice. We can choose to be happy regardless of the circumstances we find ourselves in, even if we don't particularly like them. Because happiness is not something 'out there' that happens to us or that we have to chase. Our happiness does not depend on anyone or anything, except our own choosing. It is a state of being – our natural state of being – and one we can all learn to access at any time, no matter what is going on around us. A 'state of being', whether of joy, love or happiness, comes from inside ourselves. We do not need anything else. Of course, having our basic human needs met – food, warmth, shelter, love, companionship – makes it easier but we can, if we truly desire to do so, achieve it regardless.

By learning to find joy and beauty, even if it is in only a tiny way, we slowly expand our happiness muscles and gradually find it easier and easier to see it everywhere. Even on our darkest days we can, if we really want to, find something to feel joy in. I was told the story of a young woman who was in the middle of a very painful and traumatic relationship break-up. She was finding it impossible to find any joy in life or any glimpse of light. Then a friend suggested to her that every day she could make the conscious decision to look for something, just one thing, no matter how tiny, that she could feel a sense of happiness about, even if just for a moment. The next day, filled with anger and grief, this young woman was feeling that things could not get any blacker – and then she remembered her friend's words. That was the turning point. She made the decision to be happy.

It *was* a tiny thing. She watched a raindrop trickling down the window pane and saw how beautiful it was. From there, slowly, slowly, she began to turn her thoughts and feelings – and as a result, her life – around.

POWER THOUGHT

True happiness only and always comes from within

I'm sure everyone knows the story of Cinderella. A fairy tale it may be, but every fairy tale is based on a fundamental human truth. In the story, Cinderella is oppressed and ill-treated by her step-mother and step-sisters. Now, who would have blamed her for becoming a victim, feeling miserable, blaming everyone for her situation and spending her time moaning about her lot? But instead, Cinderella chooses to live in joy and love (with, yes, an occasional moment of sadness). When we are genuinely happy and not resisting What Is things improve. The Law of Attraction says they must. In this case Cinderella's fairy godmother (Source/the Universe) fulfils her deepest heartfelt wishes and she lives happily ever after with her Prince Charming.

I think it is important to differentiate between unhappiness and feeling sad. They are not the same thing and do not emit the same energy vibrations. Unhappiness is all-pervading. It affects everything, colouring every aspect of our life. Unhappiness is rooted in unresolved issues and emotions.

Sadness on the other hand is much less all-encompassing. We can be happy yet sad at the same time but we can never be simultaneously both happy and unhappy. Sadness is a natural emotional response to something that has happened. Unhappiness has forgotten the cause and become something bigger, darker and less focussed. The expression 'joy tinged with sadness' is frequently heard. Joy tinged with unhappiness? No. I, like many other people I'm sure, have experienced the joy tinged with sadness feeling. My dad died when I was 7 ½ months pregnant with my second child. I was deeply saddened and grieved for him and yet I was not unhappy. How could I be when I had the joy of a new baby growing within me? This is sadness and happiness co-existing.

Happiness is an emotion – and our emotions are created by our thoughts. We can choose what thoughts we think and if they don't serve us, we can choose to change them. So, if you are feeling down and blue, think of something that makes you feel all warm and fuzzy inside – a memory, a favourite place, or your grandchild's smile. Knowing that we – and only we – are in control of our own happiness, knowing that no-one and no-thing can affect it unless we allow it, is powerful and empowering. We can choose to be happy, or we can choose to be unhappy. Once we know this and make our choice, then with perseverance, dedication and the desire to change, we can do so.

Be happy not good

Perhaps one of the most joy and life stifling things we ever learn is to be good, to always put other peoples' need, desires and agendas first, to be liked and approved of, to do our 'duty', to do what is 'right'. Can I suggest that you stop doing this? RIGHT NOW! Try being happy, rather than good, and see how much lighter and brighter life becomes.

Teaching us to be good is an attempt at controlling us. At getting us to conform to others' ideas of how we 'should' be thinking, doing, saying, feeling. *Being*. But it doesn't work. It can't. All that happens is that we spend our lives running around in circles, feeling increasingly 'bad' and 'unworthy' for not meeting other people's expectations. (And who decides what 'good' is anyway?). We will never succeed. We will never please everyone all the time. We can't. Everyone has their own unique needs and desires. Invariably, in trying to keep friend 'A' happy, we upset friend 'B'. Or in trying to please Mum, we upset Dad. Or, by tying ourselves in knots to keep everyone else smiling, we end up in a resentful, exhausted heap. And I'm sure every one of us has known someone whose approval was so important to us but for whom, no matter what we did and how hard we tried, nothing was ever good enough.

Being good, pleasing others has at its basis a need to win their love and approval. It assumes we aren't good enough, loveable or worthy enough just as we are. And we are. We are absolutely good enough, we are totally worthy and deserving of love and respect just because we exist. We are all fragments of Source – how much more worthy and deserving do we need to be? The more we fail in our attempts to please, which we frequently do, the more the message that we are undeserving and 'not good enough' is reinforced. We are in Fear mode again – fear of losing love, money, friendship, respect, approval or any number of other things. It strips us of our self-belief and our power. Our disempowerment creates resentment, anger and depression in us, which further reduces our joy in life and leads to physical and mental disharmony. It stops us acting as our wonderful, authentic Self, stifling our potential, our dreams and our joy in life. We begin to believe that everyone else and all their needs, dreams and agendas are more important than our own. Which they most definitely are not. As important maybe, but not more so.

POWER THOUGHT
Being good and feeling good are two very
different things

Now for the good news. Living to be happy, putting yourself and your needs first is liberating and empowering. Forget what you have learned. It's great to be selfish, with a wonderful joyful selfishness that allows us to be our true, powerful and loving Self, to reach for our dreams and to fulfil our potential. I know this goes against the grain for many people. We have received the messages for so long that we should 'do our duty' or the 'right thing' that it is hard to accept that putting ourselves first is OK.

Actually, it's more than OK. It's vital for our health, happiness and well-being. Putting ourselves first doesn't mean we have to become uncaring, uncompassionate, heartless and unfeeling. Instead, by coming from a place of love rather than fear, with a life filled with joy, we find we have more to give – and we give for all the 'right' reasons. We help and serve others not for acceptance, approval or reward or out of duty, but from love, asking and expecting nothing in return.

If you have ever been on an aeroplane, I am sure you remember the safety briefing? If the oxygen masks fall, put on your own before helping anyone else. Why? Because if you don't, you may be able to help perhaps one or two other people before needing help yourself. See to your own needs (put on your own mask) first and you will be in a position to help as many others as need it. To mix my metaphors, it is far easier to give from a full purse than an empty one.

I know some of you will be reading this and getting extremely indignant. Oh, that's OK for her to say but she doesn't have my responsibilities/ a sick husband/wife who need full time care/ a handicapped child/ my demanding boss... You can fill in the blanks. No, I don't. But let me share this story with you.

I had a sister, ten years younger than me, who had learning difficulties and would never be able to live independently. She could be a bit of a handful at times and needed almost constant supervision. When she was 18, my Dad died of cancer, aged only 55. Which left my Mum grieving for her much-loved husband and also caring for a demanding daughter. I was living in another part of the country with a new baby and my other sister was in a similar situation, so we were unable to be of much support. Although Mum had lots of love and help from friends and other family, she was finding it increasingly difficult to cope and was becoming ill. She was adamant that my sister shouldn't go into care but eventually had no option. The result – my sister moved into a great home with very caring staff and was just as happy there as she would have been at home. Mum was able to recover and start enjoying life again, travelling abroad for the first time and meeting new friends. My sister sadly passed on a few years ago but Mum is still going strong. Yes, Mum wanted to keep my sister at home with her but there was also a great sense that she 'should', that it was 'wrong' in some way to put herself first. And yet my sister was happy and had many friends in her new home. So it was a win-win situation.

This is the way in which Source works. Self-sacrifice, acting out of duty, obligation or for approval has no place in a loving Universe. When we feel these things are necessary, it is because we don't trust that Source can come up with a happy outcome for everyone. Yet Source created the world and all the marvellously intricate interactions and symbioses within it. In comparison to this complexity, to Source our issues are simple and relatively straightforward. If we believe that there is a perfect win-win situation and that Source is bringing it to us, that is what we will receive. And it will always be for the highest good of everyone concerned since Source always meets everyone's needs fully.

To anyone reading this book who believes they can only be happy while putting everyone else's needs first, please ask yourself 'Why?' Ask yourself honestly, 'Am I coming from a place of love or do I need to be seen as 'good' and deserving? Do I believe I need to earn love and approval?' What beliefs have you absorbed over the years that cause you to think you are less worthy or deserving than anyone else of having your own needs met and reaching for your own dreams?

POWER THOUGHT

'Don't ask what the world needs. Ask what makes you come alive and then go and do that. Because what the world needs is people who have come alive'

- Howard Martin

Key 5

Rediscover your True Self

Most of us have forgotten what it is to be a spiritual being. We have squashed, denied and hidden our spiritual Self for so long that we no longer remember its existence. And yet, above everything else, that is what we are, each and every one of us – a child of Source, a god or goddess in our own right. We cannot repress or eliminate our spirituality because it is the essence of our being. This physical body, this flesh and blood envelope that we identify as 'me' is just a costume, put on for this lifetime. Granted, it is a very important element of us in our current physical experience but we existed before we were born into this world and we will continue to exist after we leave it. Our spirit, our Soul, is eternal. That part of us always remembers who we truly are and where we have come from. Even when we are entirely consumed and absorbed in this game we call life, our Soul is always connected to our 'home', to Source. We can call it many different things – our Spirit, our Soul, our Higher Self – but each of us has it and each of us can learn to reconnect with it.

The Western world may be immensely rich in monetary terms, but we live in growing spiritual poverty. Unhappiness, lack of fulfilment, discontent and fear are increasingly the order of the day. We have abandoned our spirituality in favour of materialism and science. We demand that everything is black *or* white, yes *or* no, this *or* that. If it cannot be explained, proven or replicated by science we refuse to accept the possibility of its existence. The concrete and provable takes precedence over the unseen and mysterious and relegates it to fantasy, however strongly its presence is felt. Take any form of energy healing: Reiki for example. It cannot be tested, explained, reproduced or otherwise verified by scientific means (yet!). Does that mean it doesn't exist? You just need to experience its power first hand to know, without a shadow of a doubt, that it does.

While materialism and science may bring us some temporary relief and we can ignore the cries of our soul for a while, it doesn't last. It cannot. The rampant consumerism of our society is like comfort eating, filling our lives with a substitute for what we really need. Yet, even as we know deep within ourselves that these things cannot sate the hunger inside of us, still we chase more of the same. So the hole, the hunger remains. No matter how hard we try to cover it up and to satisfy our longings in other ways, it will not be silenced.

For a very long time we have tied spirituality to religion. However for growing numbers of us, religion does not sit happily. We see the dichotomy and the contradictions. We see the pain and suffering and death caused in the name of religion and we don't want anything to do with it. So we bury our deepest, most fundamental needs, stifling the calls, searching for fulfilment in any other way we can find – through accumulating material goods or money, through food, or work, or anonymous meaningless sex – or any of a thousand other ways. And it just doesn't work.

It is time to distinguish between spirituality and religion. They are not the same thing, although when they do meet it is a very happy marriage. As the saying goes 'Spirituality was created by God; religion was created by man.' Personally, I have met many committed 'religious' people who do not demonstrate an ounce of what I understand true spirituality to be all about. There was example on the news not long ago of a priest who conducted a blessing service for two of his gay colleagues in the clergy. The uproar from his fellow priests, condemning his actions, would have been funny if it wasn't so tragic. This priest displayed a true deep spirituality of non-judgement and unconditional love (probably well aware that his career may have been on the line).

His critics (many of them his colleagues) did anything but. Similarly, I have met many enlightened and profoundly spiritual people who cannot and do not ascribe to any organised religion. Their spirituality is personal, meaningful and practical.

There is a groundswell of people who are beginning to look for a deeper meaning to their lives. They are examining their values and their beliefs and accessing their inner knowing. In doing so they are re-discovering their own personal spirituality and strengthening their own unique connection to Source. They understand that the old ways of looking at things just don't work any more – if they ever did.

I firmly believe that, without a radical rethink, organised religion has had its day. We are taking responsibility for our own spirituality. We are no longer prepared to listen to others dictating what God is or isn't, or what God wants or doesn't want from us.[1] We are no longer willing to accept without question others' beliefs, fears and prejudices (all of which permeate the old organised, patriarchal religions, as well as some of the 'new age' philosophies). We are looking for the answers within ourselves – and we are finding them. We are looking into our own hearts and souls, discovering our own truths about the world and making our own ever-stronger connection to the part of ourselves that is Source – a direct line to the divine. And in doing so we are turning many of the accepted traditional teachings on their heads. No-one is right in this and no-one is wrong. Each person's spiritual truth will be different – and that's OK! The most important thing is to re-discover that connection and use it.

POWER THOUGHT
We can only satisfy our spiritual hunger by listening
to our Soul

Take responsibility for your own spirituality

This hunger for a greater spiritual awareness and understanding in our Western culture is growing. More and more people are becoming aware of an emptiness, a need for more than our materialistic society can give, a realisation that there is, after all, something 'bigger' than us. Some are turning back to traditional religions but many more are turning away, knowing that for them it is not the answer. The ancient texts and teachings have been relayed and re-(mis-!)interpreted so many times, like a centuries-old game of Chinese whispers. The dogma and the rituals no longer ring true. Instead, people are turning inside to their own inherent knowing. It is hard to do this. It is a revolution against accepted societal and cultural norms. It is breaking all the rules. Good! Rules are meant to be broken. Taking responsibility means doing what is right and authentic for you, regardless of the opinions and beliefs of others.

When I was running guided meditation sessions in our local church hall a couple of years ago, the vicar asked me to call on her. During our meeting, she asked what the sessions involved. When I mentioned that we sometimes connected with our guardian angels and guides, she was horrified, telling me in no uncertain terms that we had no right to do that, that we were playing with things we didn't understand and that we were in danger of being tempted by Satan. Then she told me that she wasn't happy with us using the hall for these meditations, asked us to find somewhere else and said that she would pray for our souls. I sat there feeling somewhat confused (I firmly believe that the Angels are beings of pure light and love whose sole purpose is to help us), bemused (was I in 21st century England or 17th century Spain?!) and amused. As I left, I silently thanked her for her genuine concern for my spiritual wellbeing – and thanked the Universe for showing me how fearful organised religion is of losing its power over its flock. Which is exactly what is happening.

We can only truly satisfy our hunger for spiritual fulfilment by listening to our Soul and establishing our own truths. By being responsible for our own spirituality. No-one else can do this for us because no-one else's reality is the same as our own. For some, it may still lead to a linking-in with a more traditional form of religion. There is nothing wrong in that. Traditional religion still fills a need – if it didn't, it would not exist. But in turning to these religions, those who have the confidence and belief to follow their own hearts will not follow the teachings slavishly but will question, meditate, accept what feels right and discard what does not. Happily, there are an increasing number of ministers in the various churches who are recognising and encouraging this change. Many of the more ancient 'pagan' traditions, which in my view relate much more closely to who we truly are and where we have come from, accept this individuality and self-responsibility as a right. Any book, workshop, seminar or teacher worth its salt will do the same. Beware of those that lay down in tablets of stone what is 'right' and acceptable, and what is 'wrong' and unacceptable. Everyone's spirituality, everyone's truth is different. One size definitely does NOT fit all.

POWER THOUGHT

Acquire the courage to believe in yourself. Many of the things that you have been taught were at one time the radical ideas of individuals who had the courage to believe what their own hearts and minds told them was true, rather than accept the common beliefs of their day.

- Ching Ning Chu

Spirituality has little to with dogma, dictates and edicts and everything to do with self-knowledge and an open heart and mind. Is the Dalai Lama less spiritual than the Pope because he isn't a Roman Catholic? Or Sir Bob Geldof any less spiritual than the Archbishop of Canterbury?

True spirituality comes from within and not from without. Instead of looking for someone else to give you all the answers, look inside. By all means read widely, listen, attend workshops and seminars. Absorb a wealth of wide-ranging ideas. Then go within, listen to your heart and your Soul and accept that which resonates with you. In some part of your being, you will know, without a shadow of a doubt, what your truth is. You will know that you have always known it and have just forgotten. Then discard what is left.

So, if we truly are spiritual beings so absorbed in playing with physicality that we have forgotten our true nature, how do we rediscover and honour it? The simple answer is, 'In any way that feels right to you'. However, I know from experience that many people who are trying to find their way back to themselves just do not know where to start. And that is what this whole book is about – a toolbox of invitations and suggestions to help you awaken your wings. Remembering our wings and remembering our true nature are one and the same thing.

Get to know your spiritual Self
Welcome silence & solitude
We live in a world of noise – most of it created artificially. By us! All day and every day it surrounds us. Occasionally we can escape it for short periods but most of the time we live bombarded by noise and distractions. We have incredibly busy, noise-filled lives – travelling to and from work each day, spending our working hours in offices or workplaces with other people, machinery, computers and telephones. Our mobiles are constantly on (and ringing!) and when we get home we immediately switch on the television, radio, music system or PC. Even those people who have the good fortune to live in more peaceful areas are not totally immune. I well remember walking through

an idyllic peaceful Northumberland valley with my young family and only the sheep and birds for company when the tranquillity was suddenly and brutally shattered by the ear-splitting roar of a low flying fighter jet on exercises. I have experienced the same thing in the peace of the Welsh mountains and in the Lake District.

Many of us live this way because we want to, choosing busy, over-filled, sound-laden lives. We could live more quietly, simply and peacefully but opt not to. I know so many people who cannot stand the sound of noiseless-ness. If they are in company they will talk to fill any silence. The TV or radio is on constantly (especially when they are alone) 'just for company'. And yet, if we cannot be happy and at ease with our own company, whose can we be happy and at ease with?

Don't get me wrong, I love music and wouldn't be without my TV or phone, but I also love peace and silence. Why is it that so many of us don't? Because we are afraid of it. Afraid of being alone with our thoughts and feelings. Afraid that if we stop the busy-ness and external diversions these thoughts and feelings will make themselves heard. We are so afraid of that emptiness and silence and yet it is only when we are truly alone and still that we can hear our own soft inner voice, get to know our True Self and discover who we are – both in the larger spiritual sense and in this physical body. It is only then that we can truly hear and understand the whispers.

Being busy, always having someone around or having 'noise' to occupy our minds distracts us from this scary prospect. Scary because this is the time when we may well come face to face with our truths. Along with our joys, loves and dreams we may meet our fears, our dissatisfaction and discontent, our hurt and pain. In silence and solitude we can no longer bury and ignore them. They bubble to the surface to be dealt with and released. This is so crucial to our well-being. Burying and denying our emotions and painful thoughts doesn't work in the long term. They make their presence felt, subtly at first and then more and more power-fully until they manifest as crises in our lives or physical dis-ease and life-threatening illness in our bodies.

Facing our fears and pain is healing, if difficult. When we confront them, deal with them and let them go we can leave them behind and move on, freer and empowered. We get to know, understand and love ourselves and rediscover our buried hopes and dreams. We grow and our lives become happier.

Stillness and solitude give us other gifts. We open up to positive emotions like love, joy and gratitude when we take the time to stop and appreciate all that is around us. We hear divine guidance more clearly and our intuition speaks more clearly. We gradually see that we are so much more than we have ever believed. And we allow the natural flow of wellbeing into our lives, bringing us all the wonderful gifts Source has to offer us. We see past the illusion of our lives to what is beyond.

Once you start to make time, space and silence for yourself, you will come to realise it is as essential to your wellbeing as eating, sleeping and breathing. You will love and crave solitude in your day and find that, no matter what else is going on, you make time in your hectic daily schedule to be alone and still, to step back from this crazy physical existence and reconnect with your inner essence.

Meditation & Time Out
A favourite way of experiencing this peace and stillness is through meditation and I love to meditate. Meditation doesn't have to involve sitting cross-legged on the floor gazing at a candle flame and chanting 'Om' – although that can be a wonderful experience. There are probably as many ways of meditating as there are people practising it and as long as it works for you, that's all that matters. I tend to meditate sitting on my sofa listening to relaxing music, sometimes with my crystals, but you can use any way that stills your mind and relaxes your

body. It is something you should find gentle, calming and that absorbs you completely. It could be as simple as stroking your dog or cat, listening to beautiful and inspirational music (and not doing anything else at the same time), gazing at the ocean or the stars or the clouds, or the flickering flames of an open fire. Or take yourself off for a long, lovely solitary walk (take the dog too!), soak in a hot bubble bath or have a facial or gentle aromatherapy massage. Of course, these things aren't pure meditation but they do allow you to access a meditative state, where your brainwaves alter. Just allow your mind to clear of the million and one thoughts and trivialities of the day, not thinking of anything much, allowing thoughts to drift through your mind, watching them detachedly without getting caught up in them. This is the time your Eureka moments come along.

Of course, if you can get into the habit of practising a more focussed form of meditation regularly, in whatever way suits you, the benefits are even greater. You can attain deeper states of relaxation, tune in even more strongly to guidance and your intuition and in that wonderful state of 'no-thought' you become so much more powerfully aware of the reality behind the illusion. If you want a more structured practice or to learn one of the traditional meditation disciplines, then go for it. Be wary however, of anyone who says his/her discipline is the only true way, or the best way or that any other way is unhealthy, unspiritual, not real meditation – or even dangerous!

The physical benefits of regular meditation for your overall health and wellbeing are well chronicled. It eases stress and tension, encouraging deep relaxation; it allows us to switch off for a while from our constant mind-chatter; it boosts the body's own self-healing mechanisms and gives us a more balanced perspective of what is going on in our lives. When I used to lead group meditations the change in the energy of the room when everyone was in deep meditation was palpable. It was beautiful and calm, yet vibrant and uplifting. I could feel everyone's vibrations as they rose and harmonised and there was total peace and light in the room.

We need this silence and solitude to hear the whispers and feel the nudges of the Universe. Without it, it's a bit like trying to hear a radio playing at low volume in a busy room. Everything else going on around drowns it out. Sit in the room quietly by yourself with the same radio at the same volume and it becomes so much more audible. Our guides and helpers, spirits and angels are answering our questions and our prayers all the time, giving us the guidance and information we ask for. But unless we grant ourselves the time and the peace, we cannot hear them.

Hear the whispers & feel the nudges
Each one of us has access to all the help and guidance we will ever need. We just don't realise it. And even when we do, we find it so very hard to hear. This help, this guidance comes to us in the form of feelings and ideas. It is our intuition, our inner knowing, our inner wisdom. Call it what you will. It comes from deep within and is that endless, limitless, be-everywhere-at-once part of us that sees every aspect and instantly comes up with the best solution and best plan of action in any individual moment through its strong, pure and constant connection to Source.

We can access it in so many ways and everyone will have a favourite, the one that we hear most clearly. Some of us go deep within the stillness of meditation. Some of us converse with angels or spirit guides. Some of us connect directly with our Higher Self, which has access to all the information that exists and has ever existed (whether this relates to the past, present or future), which is all knowledge. (This is sometimes called the Akashic records.) And some of us just listen to what feels right.

There are many people (often, but not always, men) who don't believe in such a thing as intuition. But they do believe in and rely strongly on the accuracy of their 'hunches' or 'gut instinct'. Or accept the reality of 'women's intuition' but not their own.

Women's intuition is real and powerful but it isn't a gift bestowed solely on women. Everyone has it. Perhaps it is just that women are simply more comfortable accepting it and therefore better able to tune in and listen to it, as traditionally we have been considered to be less logical, less rational and more emotional than men(!). But maybe that is a discussion better left to another day.....

Every one of us is born with the ability to tap into this reservoir of wisdom. As spiritual beings it is as natural to us as breathing is to our physical form. We retain it when we incarnate so that we can hear the guidance that will lead us to the joyful wonderful lives we came here to experience. But along the way, as we grow, we start to listen more to what other people say and think, and give this more value and credence than what we intuitively know. And more often than not we act on this external information and advice, ignoring the guidance from within. Why? Usually because if we followed our hearts, we would rock the boat, not do what was expected of us. We would perhaps do things other people didn't like or want us to do, not do the 'good' or 'right' thing (according to whose opinion?).

Our Inner Guidance *always* leads us to do what is best for us – and not just what is 'good' or 'right' in the eyes of other people. Or what they think is best for us (which is invariably if unconsciously motivated by what is best for them). So family, society, religion and science tells us that our deepest truest knowing is wrong or just our imagination or even the work of the devil leading us astray. All so that we will conform. They try to prevent us becoming mavericks, because in listening to our own truths we access our power – and they are afraid.

Yet the sad thing is that if we all heeded the voice of our Soul, there would no longer be any need to fear. Everything our intuition tells us comes from a place of unconditional love and joy and leads us unerringly to what is right and best for us. When we come from a place of love and follow our own bliss, we allow others to do the same. We are a living example of how life is intended to be. Source always offers a win-win situation. All we need to do is be in a place where we can hear it.

What sort of place is that? A place of stillness and calm. Meditating, walking, or just being, in nature, being totally absorbed in an enjoyable activity, daydreaming, dozing, sleeping (our dreams bring us powerful messages), listening to beautiful music... All of these activities and others like them still our minds from the every day mental chitter-chatter and allow the whispers to be heard. I'm sure most of you have experienced trying to have a conversation at a party, with loud music playing and lots of other people trying to have conversations and make themselves heard as well. How well can you hear what is being said to you? Usually you catch perhaps the odd word, straining to make sense of what is being said, and often don't hear it at all. When we are surrounded by busy-ness and hubbub, hearing our inner wisdom is like trying to hear a whisper at a party.

Guidance may come to us as thoughts or images, or through a conversation with one of our 'friends in high places' (such as guardian angels or spirit guides). They may appear in the form of books, a television programme or news item, or a chance meeting with someone who can help you. Or you may feel a very strong urge to visit a specific place or take some other type of action. When you are calm and centred, when your vibrations are high, then you pick up on these signals. You hear the whispers and you feel the nudges.

I have found, quite by chance, that I am very open to my intuition when I am washing the dishes. Whether it is the warm soap-sudsy water or my mind drifting and relaxing as I gaze out of the window onto my beautiful front garden and watch the birds hopping amongst the bushes, I couldn't say, but what used to be a chore has become a pleasant time-out. These days, after numerous dashes to the living room, hands dripping, to grab a pen so that I can scribble something down before the elusive inspiration disappears, I have a pen and paper to hand in the kitchen. And these insights have always been incredibly helpful.

All(!) you have to do then is trust yourself. Trust that you are really receiving this guidance, that it is not just your 'imagination'. Having learnt to do this, how do you then know if it is really coming from your inner knowing, or from your Ego, which loves to get in on the act but which never quite leads you in the best direction? Firstly, ask yourself if the guidance is coming from a place of love. Your intuition will always and only send messages that are positive, loving and empowering. If they are not, if they are coming from a place of discomfort (or fear), it's your Ego calling. Our Ego is that part of us that likes to control us and keep us in check, keep us in fear. It is essential to our day to day functioning but has been given too much power and in its desire to protect us, it stifles us. If the message is life-enhancing, accept it and act on it. If it is life-stifling, reject it. In time you will learn to recognise easily the true voice of your inner wisdom – and it will never let you down. It will lead always to the best possible action for your easiest path.

Sadly, because of the way most of us grew up and the lessons we learned, we find it really hard to tune in – and even harder to trust what we hear. 'Am I just making it up/imagining it?' 'How do I know if what I felt/thought/heard was real?' Trust that it is real, that you aren't 'just making it up'. Feel its truth, deep inside and feel the love within that truth. If the guidance you receive does seem to lead you down a difficult path it is never because it's out to give you a hard time but that you haven't quite understood the message. We have for so long buried and feared our intuitive voice that we have either forgotten its existence or become deaf to its guidance. So when we do start paying attention, it is natural not to hear accurately to begin with. Maybe things go 'wrong' and we hear the wrong message or misunderstand the whispers. Or our Ego gets in the way and we mistake its voice for that of our intuition. Happily, practice makes perfect and if we persevere we become more and more tuned in, more and more open, more and more clear. Tune into your intuition at every opportunity. Listen to it. Act on it. Trust it.

For a very long time I couldn't hear my inner wisdom, and when I began to I still believed I was imagining it all. But in my life now, I make most of my decisions based on where it leads me regardless of what 'logic' and 'reason' might dictate (although Ego and intellect do still muscle in occasionally!). I live my life by listening to my intuition. Yes, I do gather together the information I need before I make up my mind but the final decision is always what feels right. My life is flowing more easily than it ever has. And on the occasions when I don't listen to my inner guidance, I invariably find myself taking a much harder route.

If all this sounds a bit airy-fairy and hit-and-miss, think about this. Archimedes had his Eureka moment and discovered his 'Principle' while soaking in the bath. Isaac Newton was relaxing under an apple tree when the Law of Gravity 'hit' him. Einstein offered *'elegant arguments and conclusions based on physical intuition'*[2] and perfected his Theory of Relativity by daydreaming about riding on a beam of light. The most successful businessmen have a finely-honed 'gut instinct'. They just 'know' when something is right. As do many policemen. Call it intuition and they would run a mile. Call it a hunch or gut instinct and they will happily agree.

POWER THOUGHT

The intuitive mind is a sacred gift and the rational mind is a faithful servant. We have created a society that honors the servant and has forgotten the gift – Albert Einstein

---

But if all the answers are within us and we don't need anyone else, where does that leave a book like this? The answer is that it is part of the huge wealth of resources that Source is now making available to us. So many teachings, books, seminars and other channels of knowledge are being created. All are gifts from Source and all are appearing to help people re-awaken their wings. Read avidly, attend workshops and seminars – but also go within. Then be selective. Never take anything just because someone else says that it is the right way. Go within. See if it resonates with you. Do you just *know* that it's right? That is how I have proceeded throughout my journey – taking the things that I know are right for me and discarding the rest.

Once we come back to Source, we have available to us resources beyond our wildest imagining. The natural wellbeing that is our birthright begins to flow, bringing wonderful things into our lives and allowing life to flow smoothly in its turn. We tap in more strongly to our intuition and to higher guidance – and we see more clearly the gifts, signals and opportunities being offered to us. We start to understand our true power – to create, to heal, to love. We see more clearly the joy, love and beauty around us. The more we reconnect with our Souls, and consequently with Source, the clearer and stronger our own truths – and our wings – become.

Key 6

Let it flow

Stop the struggle

Flow is life. It is the free and constant movement of Source energy; a river of wellbeing that never stops and is always available to us no matter where we are or what we are doing. Flow is the effortless way a seed grows or an eagle soars. It is the constant cycle of birth-death-rebirth and renewal. It is how our bodies heal a graze and grow our hair with no intervention on our part. Flow is serendipity and synchronicity, all those things we consider to be miracles. It brings us the right people and information just when we need them. It allows us to compose a hauntingly beautiful melody, those inspirational words that flow onto the page or the flawless golf shot.

We are all connected to the Flow. Always. It's just that because the illusion of struggle is so powerful and appears so real, we don't realise that we are. And because we don't know that we are able to open up to it or how to do so, we believe that the only way to achieve success is to strive for it.

Like a lot of us, possibly most of us, I grew up absorbing the beliefs that life isn't easy, that we have to work our socks off if we want to make anything of ourselves, that wealth and success demand sacrifice. And do you know what? I've realised it just doesn't have to be true. I know there are people, perhaps a good many people, who will have an issue with that. And they will be the people firmly immersed in the 'life is a struggle' illusion, who have worked long and hard and given up a great deal to get where they wanted to be (or who, despite their best efforts, have still *not* got there). But, although it may be very hard to accept, this is a choice, just like everything else in life. We can choose to pursue success by striving, struggling and sacrifice. Or we can open up to allow success to flow to us easily and joyfully.

'Go with the flow' has become a bit of a catchphrase – and it is a great piece of advice. What does it mean though and how exactly do we do it?

When we go with the Flow, we allow ourselves to be carried along in the flow of life. We know that in this moment everything is exactly how it needs to be (even if it is not how we would choose it to be) and that everything is working to bring us to our desired destination – or an even better one. We can strive and effort, battling against the circumstances and setbacks we encounter until eventually we arrive exhausted and burnt out (if we actually get there). Or we can accept where we are and what is currently happening in our life, focussing only on where we want to go, trusting that Source has it all in hand, and allow ourselves to be guided there easily.

POWER THOUGHT

You don't have to make it happen. You just have to let it happen.

Abraham, a non-physical group of beings channelled by Esther Hicks[1], describes life as a river, where we all get in our little boats and start paddling like mad upstream, wearing ourselves out in our struggle against the current (Flow). 'Why?' asks Abraham. Why would we want to be fighting our way upstream when everything that we could ever want is downstream and all we have to do to reach it is to ship our oars, lie back, relax and allow the current (Flow) to carry us there.

As I understand it, there are two aspects to the Flow. The first is as discussed above, the general and continual flow of wellbeing through every part of the Universe. But I also believe we are able to tap more specifically into it. This is what gives us our peak experiences, our Eureka moments, those brief intervals when time stands still and the rest of the world disappears. Athletes call this the Zone, when everything comes together and magic happens. Something bigger takes over.

I remember watching an episode of a pro-celebrity dance competition on television not long ago. One of the competitors, an actor, and his professional partner had just completed a foxtrot which had moved him to tears. It had been close to perfection but it wasn't just knowing that he had danced so well that had caused him to become so emotional. After months of training and weeks of competition at last everything had come together and for the first time he had stopped trying so hard, simply letting the music carry him and his body flow with his partner's. It was the feeling of effortless ease that had so affected him.

When I think of this aspect of Flow I'm always reminded of the first Star Wars film, where young Luke Skywalker is training to be a Jedi knight. He is set a specific training task to undertake whilst blindfolded. We see him concentrating, focussing and trying as hard as he can. Yet each time he fails, until Yoda – his training master – utters the famous phrase 'Feel the Force, Luke.' Luke is to stop trying and striving and instead just feel the Force moving effortlessly through him, allowing it to guide him. Only when he does this, when he lets go, gets out of his own way and trusts in the Force's (Flow's!) power can he succeed in accomplishing the seemingly impossible.

One of the most celebrated people to go with the flow was Albert Einstein. As a physicist he worked with the scientific and provable. But in seeking his answers, *'in order to access true genius and formulate the theories that would transform the way we perceive the universe, he said he would close his eyes, relax, and "go into the still, dark place where God is."'* [2] We receive the simplest and most effective solutions once we let go of the problem and hand it over to the Universe. It was also Einstein who said that a problem cannot be resolved on the level at which it was created. To find the solution to a problem that has arisen on the physical plane, we need to look elsewhere.

When I first sat down to write this book – a long held dream – I spent a lot of time working on the structure, the tone and level for my target readership, trying to get it 'right'. And I got nowhere. Nothing worked, my ideas dried up and what I did write sounded contrived and unconvincing. It took a couple of objective (and blunt!) friends to point out to me that I was efforting and struggling, trying to write the way I thought I 'ought' to write, which was for me totally unnatural, rather than writing the book I wanted and just allowing it to happen. (Yes, I still fall easily back into the old learned habits without realising it.) I wasn't open to the Flow. I wasn't allowing the process to just be.

So I stood back for a couple of months and then began to write again. This time I didn't think about anything other than letting the words and ideas write themselves on the page. I was creating pages at a time, unedited, uncorrected and unstructured, just a stream of consciousness. I had stopped forcing it and struggling with it and things had started flowing. They always do. Now, if I pick up my pen and nothing happens, I shrug my shoulders, put it away and do something else. The words will come another day.

POWER THOUGHT

Your task is not to forge the path but to follow the path
that is revealed to you

The downside of striving

But surely we should keep trying? Isn't that a praiseworthy trait? We all know the saying 'If at first you don't succeed, try, try, try again' and heard the virtues of perseverance extolled more than once, particularly if, like I did, you attended Sunday School as a child. And there does seem to be something noble and courageous about keeping going in the face of any number of obstacles, like a salmon battling up the seemingly impossible waterfalls of a Scottish river. But the salmon is driven by primal instincts, compelled to return to its birthplace to spawn – and then die, exhausted by its efforts!

The biggest downside of 'trying' is that it creates resistance and blocks the Flow. The more we strive for something, the more resistance we create and the more elusive success becomes. Trying, efforting, struggling, striving – however you define it – these actions and the accompanying feelings generally emit a fairly low level energy vibration, the frequency that 'it's going to be tough'. It also embraces the fear that you may fail. Knowing what we do about the Law of Attraction, this just attracts more 'it's going to be tough' and 'I might fail' energy. It also emits the vibration of not trusting that the Universe can (or will) help and support us. And have you noticed that when you say you'll 'try' to do something, you rarely succeed? I'll *try to* be home early tonight. I'll *try to* make it to the club meeting. I'll *try to* give up smoking or chocolate or moaning about my boss. It appears that the energy vibration of '*I'll try to*' also embraces the energy of '*but I won't succeed*'.

If you keep on striving for something and you are not getting the results you desire, surely there must be a different, more productive (and easier) way? After all, while keeping on keeping on may be laudable, remember 'If you always do what you've always done, then you'll always get what you've always got'! I have personally discovered the truth of this numerous times and I have learnt that the different (more effective!) way is to let it go.

I have frequently struggled to bring things about, figure out how I could do it, how I could 'make something happen'. And either I was unsuccessful, wearing myself out in the process, or, when I eventually did achieve my goal, found it hadn't quite worked out the way I had wanted it to. Conversely, on the occasions when I've said OK, I don't know what else to do and handed it over to Source, everything has turned out well.

However, the real aim is to avoid getting into this 'stuckness' in the first place. To be really in the Flow, to work with it in the most effective way, it's far better to hand things over at the beginning rather than when we have reached the end of our tether.

Whenever we find ourselves efforting and striving, rather than allowing the Flow, we can be sure that our Ego is getting in on the act. Our Ego is an essential part of us – it is invaluable at dealing with day to day practical matters so that we can get on with our lives – but we have allowed it to become too big for its boots. We have allowed it to run every area of our lives instead of sticking to the purpose it was designed for. So it works outside its jurisdiction – and its capability. Ego works through our subconscious programming, which means it is governed not only by learned activities but also by our deep seated fears and beliefs. It tries its best to keep us safe through what it knows and usually, in doing so, it blocks and stifles us. Our Ego cannot work on a Source level because it doesn't know how. Ego likes to be in control and needs us to believe we cannot survive without it, and so it holds us in the illusion that we need to struggle. And it does its best to sabotage all our attempts to bypass it. Ego needs us to believe that we (or rather It!) are the only ones that can actually make anything happen and keep us safe. It keeps us apart, fostering the illusion of separateness from other people and everything around us – including Source – because to accept and allow the flow of Source makes Ego, at least in those instances, redundant.

When we strive – and do not succeed – it is our Ego that pushes us to strive harder and struggle longer in the illusion that this is the only way to achieve our objectives. In the introduction to her book *Freedom Is*[3], Brandon Bays gives us the analogy of being adrift in an ocean and struggling to stay afloat, exhausting ourselves and risking drowning because of it. Our struggles push away the lifebuoy that could save us if we stayed calm and still enough to allow it to drift to us. And then our dawning realisation that we had no need to struggle, that we can stay afloat quite easily by gently moving with the waves and allowing ourselves to be supported and carried.

I'd like to make it very clear however that allowing and going with the Flow isn't the same as sitting back and doing nothing. Pursuing our dreams can involve a lot of work. I've already mentioned that one of my long-held dreams was to write a best selling book. Now, I can put into practice all the powerful conscious manifestation techniques at my disposal and I can hand it over to Source again and again – which I have done – but if I don't sit down and spend the necessary time writing the words, I can visualise, affirm, 'feel' and allow until I'm ninety but I'll never have a best-seller! If I want to be a world class sportsman, or musician, or to climb Mount Everest, I need to put in the hours of necessary training. Following your dreams does require commitment, dedication and action. It may mean giving up certain things but when you remain in the Flow it will never involve sacrificing that which is truly important to you, as win-win solutions will present themselves. When you release resistance everything flows. The things you need appear just when you need them and because you are coming from a place of allowing, a place of love, trust and joy, even working long hours doesn't become 'hard' work. When you are 'in your bliss', totally engrossed in what you are doing, hours seem like minutes and work becomes play.

Going with the Flow, 'allowing', involves accepting situations as they arise, knowing that it is OK to have a problem, that there is a solution and that everything is fine. It means going with the current rather than trying to battle against it. It means knowing when you have done all you can do or need to do and then letting go and giving it to Source to deal with. Or, as is often said, 'Letting Go and letting God.' It means listening to your inner guidance and following it. And sometimes it involves doing nothing. Knowing when to wait is as important as knowing when and how to act.

Flow is change

One of the biggest fears most of us have is the fear of change – the fear of anything new or unknown. It is what holds us back from letting go and moving on, from fully moving ourselves into the Flow and leaping wholeheartedly into the void of infinite possibilities. Until the existing becomes so bad it is unbearable and the unknown is infinitely preferable to What Is, when the opportunity for change presents itself we will look at it longingly, then wistfully shake our heads, turn our backs on it and return to the old and familiar, if often uncomfortable.

Yet everything changes; sometimes slowly and imperceptibly, at other times with the force of a tidal wave. It will happen. It cannot be stopped. Change is inevitable because change is life. When it is blocked, stagnation occurs. And stagnation always leads to death and decay on some level. To live, to grow, we must embrace change.

But if this is the case, what about the Law of Attraction and our power to control our destiny? If we desire things to stay the same, won't that be what the Law of Attraction delivers us? Change is the order of the Universe and the Law of Attraction cannot contradict that. It may be that we can create 'same-ness' over and over for a while but sooner or later, we begin to desire something different, either through boredom and suffocation with how things are or because we unwittingly attract something we don't enjoy. What usually happens is that when we want things to stay as they are, we send out the 'I don't want...' signals: I don't want to have to move; I don't want to be made redundant. Which of course delivers to us exactly those experiences. We resist them harder, and more change appears (remember, what we resist, persists) and if we continue in the same pattern, our world starts to crumble, pushing us into the new.

POWER THOUGHT
Go with the Flow

As I see it, there are at least three steps to getting in back in the Flow. The first we have just looked at: *allowing*, giving up the need to 'make' something happen or to control the outcome (yes, that's good old Ego at work again). Just letting it happen in the perfect time and way. But to really sink into the effortless serenity of Flow we need to clear out all the other gunk that is clogging up the channel. We need to release the things that are keeping us stuck. Some of us are masters at this, releasing and moving on as we need to. Most of us however, find it very difficult and go through life lugging much of our past baggage with us. This then is the second aspect: *releasing*.

Clear out the junk

Clearing out. Releasing. Getting rid of anything outgrown, unwanted or unhelpful from our lives. This can be physical, mental or emotional 'stuff'. Anything that consumes and lowers our energy and stops us moving forward. In everything in life, before we can welcome in the new, we have to make space for it by clearing out the old. Whilst we are holding on to 'stuff' that is past its sell-by date, whether it's a pair of boots that we've been intending to mend for the last five years, a pair of too small jeans we *will* get back into one day or a past hurt that we can't (or rather won't!) let go of, we are leaking energy into it. We already know that we get what we focus on so by holding onto those things we are keeping them and their energy in our consciousness –and therefore in our lives. When we let go and put our attention (energy) elsewhere, we can let new people, new situations and new beliefs flow into our experience.

POWER THOUGHT
We have to clear out the old in order to make room
for the new

Clear out physical clutter:
In Feng Shui (the art of creating a beneficial energy flow in a building), the first step is always to clear out any material clutter and to clean thoroughly. Clearing out clutter allows energy to flow freely and easily and releases unhelpful energetic ties to objects, whether created because they are unloved and unwanted or because they hold us in the past. If you are feeling stuck, or lacking in get up and go in any area of your life, have a good clear out and then maybe a spring clean. Having a de-junking blitz will kick-start things and as clutter tends to congregate in the areas where you feel stuck (and vice versa), clearing it out will allow change in

Physical clutter is often linked to emotional clutter and that is why many people find it so hard to let go of. It shields and cushions us from our emotions and clearing it out can be emotionally taxing and traumatic, bringing up buried issues and repressed emotions. Whilst necessary and healing, it can be challenging. The feeling of freedom once we have done it, however, is fabulous!

Clear out emotional clutter:
Conversely, clearing our emotional junk can bring about a physical 'blitz' on our living space. I had a friend whose home during her (not particularly happy) marriage was filled with knick-knacks and gadgets that she constantly collected. Eventually she and her husband separated and she found a new partner with whom she was extremely content. Not long after he moved in with her I visited – and was flabbergasted! Whilst the house wasn't exactly minimalist – it was still a warm cosy home – almost all the gadgets and knick-knacks had gone. She told me that she just didn't want them any more. The house had gone from being dark and over-cluttered to light, bright and airy.

Emotional clutter can be anything from nursing old hurts and grievances, repressed emotions, fears or unhelpful and incorrect beliefs to living in the past or holding onto yearnings and hope for relationships that have long since ended (or that haven't but have far outstayed their time). These things stop us moving forward, living life fully and being in the Flow. They colour the way we act and feel and can distort our view of What Is.

Emotional clutter can sometimes be hard to release and it may be helpful to have someone to support us in doing so, whether it is a trusted friend or therapist. But it is worth doing, as it is above all our emotional clutter that limits us, our potential and our journey through life.

Clear out mental clutter:
Mental clutter is a symptom above all of our modern lifestyle but it is one we can free ourselves from if we choose. We live constantly bombarded by information, are required to learn and remember an inordinate number of facts and skills just to be able to function in our daily lives and assailed by demands from all quarters. One of the most prevalent modern-day ailments is stress – and yet stress isn't an actual thing, or a disease in its own right. Stress is created in our minds (and then shows up as

physical and mental dis-ease) because of the way we react to what is going on around us.

There are several possible solutions. a) We could take ourselves off to a cave or desert island and cut ourselves off from the world. But if we are locked into the stress reaction, we'll find things to get stressed about even here. b) We can put up with it – not really a helpful solution as constant stress will cause dis-ease and shorten our lives. c) Or we can decide that we are simply not going to play the game.

Do you know someone who gets in a tizz at everything? Or conversely someone who, no matter what life throws at them, remains calm, positive and serene? The first person lets stress rule their lives. The second person knows that stress is self-created and refuses to allow it to take root.

POWER THOUGHT

Stress does not exist except through our perceptions

Remember, stress is not a thing. It is *not* caused, as we tend to believe, by events but by our reaction to those events. The physical symptoms we experience as stress are created by a physiological reaction to our feelings. When we feel 'stressed', our bodies go into fight or flight mode, releasing adrenalin into our bloodstream and preparing for action. But with modern day stress there is no action, just more of the same, so the adrenalin remains flooding around our bodies and exhausting our cells. If we can change our emotions, by changing our reaction to what we perceive as stressful situations, we can stop the release of this adrenalin and the ensuing physical effects. How? Here are a few suggestions:

Change your perspective:
'Give me the courage to change those things I can change, the serenity to accept those which I cannot – and the wisdom to know the difference'. This is known as the serenity prayer and it is excellent advice for reducing stress in our lives. Life happens, we create unwelcome experiences and fighting against What Is and what cannot be quickly changed is one of the most stress-creating activities we can undertake. Accept what is going on, allow it to be and not only are we calmer and better able to deal with it but the situation tends to get resolved more quickly and more satisfactorily. We have stopped resisting. It doesn't mean you don't care. It means you are handling it in a much more objective way.

Just say No:
There is always a huge amount of 'stuff' going on – demands on our time, on our energy and on our money. To ease stress and demands in your life, learn to say 'No'. It doesn't mean you are selfish and uncaring. It means you value yourself sufficiently to allow yourself some time and space. Simplify your life – do less. And for those of you who say you can't – you can! It's simply a matter of choice.

And all those urgent tasks that absolutely *have* to be done?
- Do them (and get them out of your head so you aren't spending energy thinking about them)
- Delegate them

or
- Ditch them. Are they really all so necessary anyway?

POWER THOUGHT
Just say No

Modern technology allows us to be available to people 24 hours a day. I know people who get in a blind panic if they haven't got their mobile phone with them. What if somebody needs to contact them? Well, they'll have to do what people have always done up until the last 10 years or so. Wait and try again later. I also know of several of my friends who get really irritated with me when they can't get hold of me exactly when they want to. I have a mobile – and unless I am expecting an important call it is usually switched off. I use it for emergencies and occasionally to call other people. For the same reason, if I am busy, or chilling out, I don't always answer my home phone. I do not feel I am obliged to be permanently available. If people need to talk to me they leave a message or send me a text and I call them back. Why not try it for yourself?

Stop worrying:
We have already seen how and why the Law of Attraction will draw to us the things we worry about. Worrying also wastes a lot of energy that we could be more effectively focussing elsewhere. Now if you are a 'born' worrier (there's actually no such thing, it's a learned behaviour) it won't be easy to change the habits of your lifetime but you can do it. By being aware, catching yourself when you are in 'worry mode' and consciously choosing more positive thoughts, little by little your patterns will change – and so will your life.

Trusting
The final aspect of Flow is trusting. It involves letting go of need, desperation and expectation and trusting that Source has it all in hand. Trusting that what you desire is already yours and is even now starting to manifest. Trusting that the Universe in its creative wisdom knows exactly the best way to deliver it to you for the highest good of everyone concerned and the best time to do so. And perhaps hardest of all, trusting that even if it does not

manifest, the process is still working perfectly and that a) there is still something you need to do or some resistance you need to clear, b) the time is not yet right or c) there is something better on its way. Once you trust that whatever you desire is already yours, when deep inside you just know it without any shadow of a doubt, then need and desperation disappear. They have to. The key is to expect without expectation. To expect what you have wished for to show up in your life at any moment, without any expectation of how or when that may be.

Going with the Flow is *not* fatalism. It isn't considering ourselves hopelessly at the mercy of Fate or an unpredictable god. Neither is it giving up. When we let go, when we surrender to Source, we send out a positive high frequency of expectation, anticipation and trust. Giving up, on the other hand, carries the vibration of hopelessness, powerlessness and disappointment. In giving up, we no longer expect to receive or to succeed. When we surrender, we know we will. In going with the Flow we set our desires clearly and then we allow: allow the Flow to carry us to them (or them to us!); allow Source to discern the best path for us to take. And we allow ourselves to open up to receive all the guidance, resources and inspiration we will ever need. We allow miracles into our lives.

POWER THOUGHT

Flow is the natural state of the Universe. Joy, love and abundance flow freely everywhere, and to everyone, constantly. Struggle is an illusion, a concept dreamed up by man and his ego. Struggle is resistance. It blocks the Flow. The harder we struggle, the more we block the flow of wellbeing into our lives.

Key 7

Live NOW

'Yesterday is history. Tomorrow is a mystery. Today is a gift.
That's why it's called the present'.

A well-known, well-worn phrase. Clichéd? Yes, probably. But
think about it, even just a little bit, and you'll see how true it is.
Yesterday *has* gone, as have all the yesterdays before it. Nothing
that we can do Now will affect or alter what occurred. We cannot
in this moment do anything 10 minutes ago (or for that matter,
an hour in the future.) Likewise, tomorrow – and all the future
tomorrows after that – have not yet arrived. What it will be
depends on what we are creating in each Now moment. Even the
most skilful and powerful manifestors know that they cannot
control every twist and turn. Neither would they want to. The
future is an unknown. That is what makes life such an exciting
roller-coaster ride.

Happiness is Now

When we feel bad, (have feelings we do not enjoy) it is usually
because we are focussing on past or future events. All feelings
are created by our thoughts and our thoughts have a strong
tendency to slip back into the past or forward to the future. By
focussing on what is happening now, in this moment, their
power fades. We can experience life as it actually is, uncoloured
by our fears and anxieties. However, our thoughts rarely reside
in the present moment without conscious effort and practice. But
if we can find a spark of happiness in this moment,.. then in this
one....and in this one... (which is actually much easier than it
sounds if we make up our minds to do it) and if it is this string

of moments that makes up our life, then by finding happiness in each 'Now' we are creating a happy life. Finding something good in each moment is not necessarily difficult. Choosing to look for it is.

We can find happiness in many forms – love, beauty and appreciation, for example – and it is rare that we are ever totally distanced from at least one of them. It's true that, when everything seems to be pushing us down, deciding to look for that spark of light can be a challenge, but once we start we begin to notice it more and more. (Clinical depression is a separate issue altogether and needs to be dealt with professionally.)

I'm sure most, if not all of us can relate to the joy that being fully present in this moment brings. Think of a time you have been totally absorbed in something – a film, a sport, a hobby – or even just lost in a magnificent view. Time appears to stand still, everything else disappears from our awareness and we feel a sense of Flow throughout our whole being. When we can learn to re-create that sense of presence at will, even tedious jobs and circumstances become easier (and often more enjoyable and interesting).

Only Now matters

Now is the only moment that counts (in fact, it is the only moment there really is). Or, as is often said, "Now is our only point of power.' It is the only moment in which we have true power – the power to act, to choose, to create our future and to manifest our dreams. No matter what has gone before, in this moment – Now – you have the opportunity to start to change things. To think, act, feel differently. Each Now is the chance for a brand new beginning. Our entire lives are simply an infinite number of Now moments strung together. And in each of these moments we have the power to choose how we feel, how we act, to choose to change things.

So, if our life is simply a series of Nows and we aren't fully present, mentally or emotionally, in those Nows, how can we be truly living? We spend our time lost in the past or the future or anywhere other than here. Always our focus is somewhere else. Life passes us by and before we know it, it's reached its end... and we're left wondering where it's gone. Our children grow up and somehow we miss it and we wonder why. Days, months, years melt into one another and we don't see them pass. We miss the beauty, love and joy that surround us in every moment. If Now is life, and we are ignoring the Now, we are ignoring life.

POWER THOUGHT
Now is the only moment that exists

To really learn how to live in the Now, just watch a young child and follow her example. When she finds something she is interested in, whether it's a caterpillar or a lollipop, she becomes totally absorbed in the experience. The wonder of the moment takes hold and nothing else exists. Then she'll move onto the next thing, and then the next, each time focussing her whole attention on what has captivated her. A child will laugh, throw a tantrum, cry and then be laughing again, all within the space of a few minutes. He feels his emotions, accepts them, allows them, releases them and moves on (all as second nature). The previous moments have no power. He doesn't go back and dwell on them. As adults, we can copy this way of being. Feeling, allowing and releasing in this way, then moving on, prevents us building up the emotional baggage we all tend to carry with us.

I know many people may argue with that, but we can. It's all a matter of choice. 'Oh, it's so much easier for children. They haven't got to cope with the stresses (that word again) of everyday life.' No, it's true, they don't (although growing up is harder than many adults accept). But the fact is that if we can learn to live more in the Now, we discover that these stresses suddenly start to diminish. Feeling bad, stressed, anxious or any of the other numerous draining emotions almost always comes from dwelling on what has happened in the past or worrying about what may happen in the future. Our minds are very good at churning this stuff over and over – and each time we do, it tends to build up into something worse. Give what you are currently doing your full attention and you won't be thinking about what your boss said yesterday or where your next mortgage payment is coming from. To repeat myself, stress is *not a thing*. It is a reaction created in our mind by our thoughts. Stop those thoughts, even for a short while, and stress eases.

Worrying about the past is pointless and useless. We cannot change anything that has happened or anything we have said. Perhaps even more pointless (and definitely more destructive, as it amplifies our negative thoughts vastly) is the 'What if...' line of thought. You know the kind of thing: your teenage daughter walks in at midnight, while you are sitting waiting for the phone call to collect her. She was bored at the party (or whatever) and decided that as it was such a lovely evening she would walk home – by herself. Immediately you go into worry overdrive. What if she had had an accident? Or been attacked or abducted? She could have been raped or murdered and you'd never have seen her again. And so on and so on. I'm not denying that tragically these things can and do happen. But in this case, it hasn't. Your child is home safe and well. There is no reason to worry.

When it comes to the future, have you noticed that when we think about the things we are anxious about, we tend to paint the blackest picture possible? We start running horror movies in our heads: we're going for an interview and we just know we'll come across like a bumbling idiot who can't string a sentence together and then we'll knock over our coffee cup and walk into the wrong loos and... Aside from pushing our stress and anxiety levels through the roof, these thoughts and fears make the outcome we dread much more probable. If we're going to dwell on future possibilities, it makes much more sense (and makes us feel a lot better!) to imagine the best possible outcome.

As adults with responsibilities of course we need to think about and sometimes plan for the future. But have you noticed that many people think about these things constantly and yet never come up with anything concrete? They think while they're driving, eating, working, socialising but in doing so are only giving it a part of their energy and attention. They are also taking that share of energy and attention away from the other things they are doing, which in turn decreases their enjoyment and satisfaction in those other things. If you have plans or decisions to make – or you just need to think about your future – give it the attention it deserves. Be present with it. Set time aside solely for that purpose and give it your complete focus. Visualise if it's appropriate. Then let it go. You'll find answers and solutions popping into your head when you least expect it.

Do less, be more

We all have immensely busy lives, overflowing with demands on our time. It frequently seems we never have enough of that precious commodity and that we are snowed under by our to-do lists. We're always rushing to get on with the next thing or to our next appointment. And in doing so, we completely bypass the current moment. One day it's Easter and the next time we look up, the leaves are changing colour in the trees and the evenings are getting darker once again. Six months or so have passed and we haven't even noticed.

I still feel frequently overwhelmed by To-Dos piling up (this relates to some residual deep seated 'life is a struggle' beliefs, which many people hold) but when I focus solely on what I am doing in the moment and forget the rest the pressure disappears. All we need to do is give our current task our full attention and energy, do it and move on to the next thing. By only seeing one task at a time rather than looking at everything else piled up behind it, it never feels so daunting. I know from experience that this technique works. We concentrate better, work more effectively – and get more done!

Remember though that no matter how long and how hard you work, your to-do lists will *never* get finished. As soon as you cross off one thing, you'll add another two or three to the bottom. Much better to surrender. SLOW DOWN! It's a great way to start really living and enjoying every moment. It is often said that we are human beings, not human doings. So do less, and just 'be' more. Do only the things you absolutely *have* to do or want to do, and forget the rest. They'll get done sometime and if they don't, so what? Sadly, many of us think we can't stop, believing we have to continue this breakneck charge through life or everything will fall apart. We *can* stop, and our lives won't collapse if we do. It's all a choice. Choose to do less. Absorb and enjoy *all* the moments.

I freely admit to still sometimes getting a bit obsessive about my to-do lists, feeling I 'have' to tick off a certain amount on them every day. It can leave precious little time for spontaneous fun activities or just taking time out. And the truth is, I don't have to do them all. Recently, when I had again fallen into my to-do list hamster wheel, I asked for guidance on how my life could flow more easily and joyfully. I received the following: *Let go of your to-do lists. Life is not lived by to-do lists, it is lived through joy, spontaneity, love and desire'.* I still have my daily list, but now it comprises at the most one or two Must Dos – and I don't stress if even they don't get done. I have a separate list (yes, I do like my lists!), I can work from if and when – and ONLY if and when – I really want to. The rest of the time I do what I want to do.

A final word on Now
Our True Self lives only in the Now. Our lives are created from an infinite series of Nows and so many spiritual sources, both ancient and modern, tell us that there is only one Now. Time, as

we know it does not exist. Past and future do not exist. Time is something that we have invented as physical beings to make sense of our existence. In the field of Physics, Einstein was the first to cast doubt on time as a linear reality when he wrote that *'Time is not at all what it seems. It does not flow in only one direction, and the future exists simultaneously with the past.'* His work was expanded and elaborated by his close friend and colleague (and, many believe, intellectual equal), Kurt Gödel. *"Gödel (...) had for the first time in human history proved, from the equations of relativity, that time travel was not a philosopher's fantasy but a scientific possibility (.....). Gödel was quick to point out that if we can revisit the past, then it never really 'passed'."* [1]

POWER THOUGHT

Time, like space, is everywhere at once. All exists at the same moment alongside itself. There is no past or future. All that exists is the present moment – Now. Now is all there is, all there ever has been and all there ever will be. There is only Now. Every moment ever experienced is Now. The past and the future have no reality except in our creation of them, our belief in them.

Key 8

Reconnect with the natural world

In the Western world, as a society we tend to live shut away from the natural world. We work in offices that are sealed off from the world around us, our fresh air coming from mechanical air-conditioning, and we drive to and from them in our car-cocoons. We live in hermetically sealed homes that are designed to keep us in an artificially controlled environment, ignoring the urgings of our bodies to listen to and honour the rhythms and cycles of Nature. One of our most popular leisure activities is shopping, and we spend much of our remaining free time in front of the television or computer or working out in gyms. Why? Why go to a gym to exercise? Why not use our bodies as Nature intended, exercising naturally in the fresh air?

The closest many of us get to Nature in the raw is our garden or local park, but even these have become so tamed and 'designed' that Nature itself has very little input any more. We are paving, gravelling and decking over our little oases to make them low-maintenance, as we don't want to spend our time working with the plants. We grow highly-bred, disease- and pest-resistant varieties and use a plethora of chemicals to eliminate any (perish the thought) lurking diseases or pests that may chance an attack. It is hardly surprising that in such an artificial environment we cannot understand the true beauty and wonder – and harmony – of Nature in the wild.

So much of our disconnection with our spiritual Self comes from our disconnection with Nature. We began to lose our way when we started to leave the countryside to live in bigger and bigger towns and cities. We slowly lost our reverence for and understanding of Nature and its processes. And, as we are part of

Nature, we also lost sight of the magic and perfection that is ourselves. We no longer revere the miracle of the first shoots pushing through the ground in Spring or the ripening of juicy apples and plums on the trees in Autumn. We no longer stand in awe at the wonder and grandeur of a powerful thunderstorm. Over the centuries we have distanced and disconnected ourselves from it more and more until it seems like a stranger to us, mysterious and frightening, and yet it is our ally. It connects us to who we are and to all that is.

Yes, I know. This may seem a poetic, romanticised viewpoint and I am well aware of the hardship and poverty suffered by country people throughout the ages. But this poverty and hardship was not created by Mother Nature, rather by their fellow men with their quest for ever more power and riches. Nature provides enough for everyone. What humankind does with this bounty is our choice.

Nature seems harsh and cruel to us sometimes. And yes, it can be harsh perhaps. Extreme, certainly. But cruel, no. That is just our 'civilised' perception. We look at the arid, oven-heat deserts or the icy, frozen 'wastelands' and see them as cruel and inhospitable because we do not understand them. We do not feel their heartbeat. But the indigenous peoples who live and breathe there do. And have for millennia. Take the Australian outback for example. To many people on Earth, particularly those of us from the more so-called developed regions, it would more likely than not be fatal to be there without food and water. To the Aborigines, everything they need is freely available. They learn and listen to the song of the land and they hear its wisdom and guidance. Likewise the Inuit of the frozen deserts of the North. Or the nomadic tribespeople of the Sahara.

It is true that life is becoming harder for these people but it is not Nature that is creating this situation. It is a disconnection and distancing from ancient knowledge. It is humankind affecting the rhythm and balance of Nature through our actions and the adoption of materialism as a pseudo-religion, all at the expense of inherent spiritual understandings. Nature is neither intrinsically good nor bad. It just is. In its turn, it too follows the cycles and rhythms of the Universe, as we all do.

This forgotten awareness of the Earth and her rhythms is a true gift of wisdom. How many of us take the time to look at a clear night sky and gaze in amazement at the millions and trillions of stars, lost for words at their magnificence and at the sheer awesome mind-blowing size of the universe? Watch a tiny seedling grow, little by little, day by day, into a tall, sturdy plant? Sense the influence of the waxing and waning of the moon? Really understand the incredible miracle of Nature's every creation? Instead, we ignore it, or take it all for granted, wantonly build on it and destroy it. We are, at least in this moment and this existence, also physical beings, animals if you like. And in exactly the same way as every other creature, we too are governed by Nature. Nature is who we are. Our physical bodies come from it and will return to it. Our cycles and rhythms are the cycles and rhythms of the natural world – the tides, the seasons, the cosmos. Yet still we cut ourselves off from it, seal it out, sterilise it. No wonder we feel so disconnected.

POWER THOUGHT
Take time to watch the sun rise

Nature is balance

Everything is Nature is perfectly balanced harmony. For every 'problem', there is a solution. Every spring, the shoots on my roses are so thick with greenfly you cannot see the leaves. By the end of May they are all but gone. I could panic at the first sight (as I used to!) and spray them into oblivion with some anti-aphid chemical, but nowadays I trust that Nature will bring things back into balance. And She does. As soon as word gets out about the feast my garden is providing, I have an army of blue tits, ladybirds and lacewings munching away until the 'pests' are gone. The same goes for our own physical ailments. For every illness and dis-ease we experience, Nature somewhere has a solution. But we ignore Her potential. What is sadder is that, with our natural resources disappearing faster than we can blink, many of these remedies may have been lost to us forever.

Nature brings us back into balance in other ways too. Her colour is green, the colour of healing, harmony and the heart chakra. She soothes and revives our bodies, minds and Souls. When we spend time outside in the natural world, we are calmed, replenished and revitalised. Whether we are standing on a windy hilltop, feeling the cobwebs being blown away, wandering along a tranquil riverbank or simply sitting in a garden amongst the flowers and bees, our bodies relax, our minds slow their constant chatter and our hearts and Souls expand. We feel we have room to breathe – and to just be. Nature nurtures us and nourishes us. That is Her gift. Yet, in our busy whirlwind lives, how many of us really take the time to notice Her, stop long enough to appreciate these gifts and hear Her wisdom?

In reconnecting with Nature, we begin to recognise the creative power and perfection of the Universe. Everything works together in perfect harmony and synchronicity. It all happens without struggle or effort, just flowing from one moment to the next. The plants don't have to force themselves to grow, the bees don't strain to fly, there is no effort in the water tumbling down the streams and rivers. Everything flows. Time has no meaning – in this world past and future do not exist. Life just *is*.

What we have forgotten is that this same creative power – the power that formed the Universe, the Earth and *everything* on it – is also within each of us. We all have this incredible ability to create, effortlessly. Once we truly know this, in our deepest centre, nothing is beyond us. It really is pretty amazing!

Getting back in touch with the natural world, whether in our gardens, by the sea shore, walking through woodland, or anywhere else, we open up to this power. We sense it, even though we may not understand what we are feeling, and it nudges our ancient hidden knowing. When we are surrounded by the great green outdoors, our spirits rise and we feel better... And as we have seen in the chapter on the Law of Attraction, feeling good is what really matters.

POWER THOUGHT
'Nature brings solace in all troubles' – Anne Frank

But how do we begin to reconnect with the natural world? It's so BIG... Simple – just get out in it. Look at it, feel it, experience it. Make time every day to reconnect with Her, even if it is just for 10 minutes or so. Here are some suggestions for simple ways to do this:

- feel the wind in your hair, the rain on your face and the sun on your skin – Nature is sensual!
- hug a tree. Or if that is a step a little too far out of your comfort zone, stroke its bark, feeling the texture, its life and the energy flowing beneath
- watch the sun rise (or set)
- take a walk in the park at lunchtime, remaining fully aware and present (leave all your worries and mind chatter at the park gates)
- star gaze
- plant some seeds in a pot and watch them as they grow (if you plant vegetable seeds you will be able to harvest them as well)

- bring the natural world indoors with flowers, plants, pebbles, driftwood and any other beautiful natural items
- become aware of the changing seasons or the phases of the moon and see how they affect you
- meditate in a safe, quiet spot outdoors
- walk in the woods, or by a lake, river or stream

Whether it's your garden, a park or a vast wilderness, each brings its own gifts and brings us closer to the power and energy of Nature. The manicured parks and gardens are calming. They can bring order and peace to jumbled thoughts. And they are safe. (Many of us have a deep-seated fear of the wildness and rawness of Nature.) In our gardens, we can meditate without being disturbed, or get our hands into the soil, the flesh of Mother Earth. We can nurture and tend our plants, watching them grow, wondering at the miracle of the process. I love to sow seeds and take cuttings, watching the magic of a whole new plant growing from the tiniest fragment. This is the power of effortless creation at work.

Pastoral areas and farmland are also relaxing because they too have, to a certain extent, been tamed. But mixed in with this, we find the gentler wildness of Nature, evident here in the hedgerows, field margins and streams.

For a real blast of deep, powerful connection, however, I believe we need the wilder, untamed areas – moors, mountains, deserts and seashore. They energise, excite, inspire and awaken. This is where I love to be, where I feel I've truly come home. Even if, in the UK at least, most of wild areas are to some extent managed, they still retain a sense of raw untouched Nature. Being in these places (especially alone) puts all cares and worries into perspective. We hear the voice of Source on the wind, or in the gurgling of a mountain stream, or in the crash of waves on a rocky shore. We see how small and fleeting our physical lives are in the scale of things and how all our problems, no matter how big and important they seem to us in the moment, are merely transient – and that they too will pass. We are surrounded by a strong sense of the ever-present Now, where past and future are meaningless.

POWER THOUGHT

Nature is effortless creation in action

For many people, however, these places are frightening and alien, far removed from the safe, controlled surroundings they are used to. I grew up near Dartmoor and spent many happy childhood days rambling the moors with my parents. But even now, much as I love the wildness and solitude of these places, I am influenced by the messages I absorbed as I grew up about the dangers and perils of venturing into such places alone. Many years later, these fear-filled warnings are still with me and yet, without wishing to promote foolhardiness and irresponsibility, I now also firmly believe that if we listen to our own guidance and to the whispers of nature, and act responsibly then we will remain safe and looked after.

This is our solution. The more we reconnect with Nature, the more we are able to reconnect with Source and our True Self. Interestingly, it also works both ways. The more we re-discover and strengthen our connection to Source in other ways, the more we feel the need to reconnect with Mother Earth. We respect Her power, but we are not afraid of it.

The Earth is our nurturer, our sustainer and our life-giver. It holds us and keeps us. The heartbeat of the Earth is our heartbeat. When we reconnect with Nature, we reconnect with something so much bigger than ourselves but that is also an essential and integral part of us. It gives us life and strength. It calms and soothes us, excites and inspires us, awakens our inspiration and allows us to see at least a glimpse of who we truly are.

Key 9

Believe the unbelievable

Anything and *everything* is possible. We can do, be and have anything we choose. We can cure ourselves of so-considered 'incurable' diseases, manifest wealth and success from nothing, travel to distant galaxies without space ships, be in two places at one time, meet angels and fairies, walk through walls... Some people claim to have done so. So why can't the rest of us? Simply because we don't believe we can – not just individually, but as a collective consciousness. As a whole. Sadly science has become the final word, particularly in the western world, and it has been drummed into us over the last couple of centuries that if something cannot be 'scientifically' proven, tested and replicated, then it doesn't exist.

The people who have achieved these feats know differently. They have total faith that such things are possible. They believe in their power. A great example of this is fire-walking. Even 20 years ago, fire-walking was usually considered a trick, an illusion of some kind, or a kind of magical feat performed by someone with unattainable mystical powers. It is simply not 'scientifically' possible for our delicate, sensitive skin to be in contact with red-hot coals for even a split second without causing serious burns and extreme pain. And yet we *can* do it. More and more people are undertaking the challenge, walking the coals and realising that all their pre-conceived beliefs have just flown out of the window. The impossible has become the possible.

For something to be truly possible for the majority to achieve, a certain number of those people, a 'critical mass', must believe – or rather know without a shadow of a doubt – that it is possible.

This is now happening with fire-walking. If the man down the road or your postman or the girl in the shop can do it, so can you. But it goes deeper than this. It is an unnoticed change in consciousness that affects everyone, regardless of whether they have knowledge of what is concerned or not. This has been called the Hundredth Monkey Syndrome.

The Hundredth Monkey Syndrome

The phenomenon was first documented by scientists who had spent 30 years observing monkeys in the wild on isolated Japanese islands. In 1952, on one of the islands, they gave the monkeys sweet potatoes that were covered in sand. Although the monkeys liked the sweet potatoes, they did not like the sand. One day, one of the younger female monkeys washed the potatoes in a nearby stream. She taught her mother and her playmates how to do it and they in turn passed on the knowledge. Apparently, between 1952 and 1958 ninety-nine monkeys learned to wash their sweet potatoes. Once the hundredth monkey learnt this, almost every monkey on the island suddenly began to wash their potatoes before eating them.

The added energy of this hundredth monkey had somehow created a behavioural breakthrough, a change in consciousness. What was more amazing was that the scientists observed that colonies of monkeys on other islands, as far as 500 miles away, had also begun to wash their sweet potatoes. The behaviour had jumped over the barrier of the sea, without any contact between the colonies.

The Hundredth Monkey Syndrome mirrors the idea of critical mass. When only a small number of people know something in a new way, it remains available to only those people. The Hundredth Monkey Syndrome theorises when this number grows to a certain level, there is a point at which if only one more person tunes in to a new awareness, this altered field of energy enters the mass consciousness so that this new awareness is absorbed by almost everyone. Gregg Braden makes the same point in a more mathematical (scientific!) way in his book *The Divine Matrix*[1] *'The minimum number of people required to 'jump-start' a change in consciousness is the √1% (the square root of 1%) of a population.'* He gives us more concrete figures – it works out at approximately 100 people in a million, or 8,000 of the world's current total population of 6 billion. These are very small numbers and are the (theoretical) minimum that is needed to start the process of change. The more people involved, the faster change can happen.

Looking at it from a different angle, even twenty five years ago, the idea on being able to access unlimited information at your fingertips within seconds, for the entire world to be connected instantaneously in an intangible 'virtual' electronic information web was the stuff of science fiction. Less than one hundred years ago, the concept of transplanting a human heart into another, living person, and for that person to go on to live a full and healthy life was just about inconceivable. Two hundred years ago pretty much no-one would have believed it possible for a machine to ever fly through the air, let alone carry millions of people around the world every year. And as for space travel and moon landings…

The field of quantum physics is turning long held beliefs about what is physically possible (and which form the basis of a great proportion of our collective consciousness) on their heads. Once firmly and solely in the realms of pure science fiction, phenomena such as bi-location – a single object being simultaneously in two separate locations – are being scientifically observed. In repeatable experiments.

And consciousness *is* changing. More and more of us are beginning to understand that we can create anything we desire. This isn't just a theoretical realisation, but an experiential knowing, perhaps on a small scale to begin with, but once people see the results of what they are doing, they can achieve anything. Because they know, without a shadow of a doubt, that they can. Open your heart and your mind. Allow untold, unthought possibilities to enter. Think beyond what has been thought, believe beyond what has been believed to be possible. Allow yourself to believe in its reality. The greatest achievements have come through visions of what might be, rather than what is. *Nothing* is impossible.

Allow yourself to believe in your wildest dreams, to desire what you truly and deeply desire. Allow yourself the life you want and deserve, however that is. The greatest gift you can offer to others is to live your truths, to show that the seemingly impossible *is* possible. By living, leading and teaching by example, you will inspire others to do the same. We are unlimited beings of unlimited potential. Once we truly understand and know that, then we step into our power. We are transformed.

POWER THOUGHT
Today's impossibility is tomorrow's reality

Key 10

Being physical

Up until now we have focussed very much on our spiritual Self, primarily because it is the part of us that we most often ignore or deny and because it is the part that we most need to reconnect with in order to re-awaken our wings. But what about the physical 'Me'? Where does that fit into all of this? Because, in this lifetime at least, we are also firmly physical beings in a physical world. It is vital to us to remember and nourish our Soul, but to deny ourselves the joys of an embodied existence is as harmful to our overall wellbeing as ignoring our spiritual Self and focussing solely on the physical and the material. To fully experience life, to fulfil our brief if you like, we need to nurture both – and that includes all the pleasures our flesh and blood bodies were created to enjoy.

Many religions and belief systems have for a very long time claimed that the only way to enlightenment is to deny ourselves these joys. Asceticism, self denial and deprivation, discomfort, pain and sacrifice have all been promoted as the only way to really 'know' God. There is no doubt that this is one way to go about it – after all, Jesus spent 40 days and 40 nights in the wilderness, the Buddha renounced his royal position and all worldly possessions to live as a monk, enduring (self-inflicted) torments for many years and in Norse mythology Odin is said to have hung upside down from Yggdrasil, the tree of life, his side pierced with his own spear, until he gained the knowledge he sought. But I can't help believing there is another, less uncomfortable route. After all, why would Source have equipped us with these incredible bodies, capable of enjoying so many wonderful experiences, if we weren't meant to use them fully? It would be a bit like being invited to a fabulous banquet, tables weighed down with delicious food, and only being allowed to eat dry bread. Source desires that we live in joy, that we experience all the delights of life. It is the only way in which it, Source, can itself experience the bliss of the physical. So in denying ourselves its joys, we also deny them to Source.

Sensuality, the pleasures of and joy in the senses, can and does sit very comfortably alongside spirituality, enhancing and deepening our experience of life. This is an earthy embodied spirituality, a spirituality that exists joyfully within the physical world, embracing it and revelling in it. It welcomes and values it all, whether the damp mistiness of an autumn morning, the delicious hot sweatiness of sex or the wild roar of a thunderstorm. This is the spirituality of our ancestors, who celebrated life, including its unseen realms, with feasting and revelry, song and dance – and irrepressible love-making afterwards in the fields and forests. They saw no boundaries between the physical and the spiritual.

POWER THOUGHT
Make a song & dance of life

However, as the organised patriarchal religions such as Christianity spread, this lusty earthy spirituality gradually disappeared. The heartfelt connection of the divine feminine was replaced with a head-based masculine view of how things 'should' be. Religious celebrations became solemn, rigid affairs (take Oliver Cromwell's banning of Christmas festivities, for example) and slowly we began to believe that it was 'wrong' to be happy and joyful. That was for the next stage – Heaven. This life was for preparing ourselves, repenting our sins, making ourselves worthy – and suffering to do so.

Happily things have changed a great deal since Oliver
Cromwell but, in England at least, the puritan ethic still remains
strong. Until very recently it was severely frowned upon to
laugh or be frivolous in church, where hushed reverence and
solemnity were the expected behaviour (and in some cases still
is!). Elsewhere in the world, there are religious belief systems
that ban singing, dancing and other forms of joyful self-
expression. Pleasure and enjoyment have taken second place to
hard work and striving, deprivation and denial. We're only half
joking when we talk about enjoying ourselves too much. We
sometimes feel we don't deserve the sensory and sensual
pleasures we thrive on or we believe it is somehow wrong to
indulge in them. We feel guilty about them. But why? If
whatever you 'indulge' in brings you joy, and is harming no-one,
how can it be wrong? We are here to experience joy and the
physical body we inhabit provides us with a myriad of ways to
do so. Now, I'm not suggesting you go out and make rapturous
love on your local hillside – although if you want to, why not? –
but isn't it about time this either/or rift between body and Soul
was dissolved once and for all?

Maybe for you, your indulgence is to sink into a hot scented
bubble bath by candlelight with a glass of good wine. Perhaps
you love to feel your body move as you run, jump or dance? Or
to taste the dark creamy coldness of chocolate ice- cream? Purr at
the firm touch of a massage sweeping the tension from your
muscles? Or lose yourself in a lover's caress? If we were not
intended to feel and enjoy all these sensations, why would we
desire them and have the capacity to receive pleasure from
them?

Of course, our physical world isn't all about pleasures 'of the
flesh', although these tend to be the ones we feel most guilt at
enjoying. We also live on a breathtakingly lovely planet, a planet
filled with beauty – both natural and man-made – for us to
appreciate. Whether we are gazing in awe at towering snow-

covered mountain peaks, captivated by the rippling notes of a clarinet or flying over the waves in a sailing boat, we are experiencing and revelling in the physical world around us. Surely it's time we started celebrating these pleasures and truly appreciating their presence in our lives once more. We have a tendency to get lost in our heads, wrapped up in the busy-ness of our lives, taking the world around us for granted. Or to believe that to be a properly 'spiritual' person we have to set aside the physical and mundane. When, in fact, the reverse is true. To fully enter the spiritual realms we also need to remain firmly grounded in our physical one. In the same way as the tallest skyscrapers have the deepest foundations, in seeking to reach the spiritual heights we need to be rooted firmly in our earth-iness.

Look after your Home

Our body is a miracle of trillions of co-operating cells that together form our home in this lifetime. It works harder than we can ever imagine, replacing, repairing and regenerating itself constantly until the moment of our death, working for the vast majority of the time in perfect balance. In fact it works so hard at this that, twelve months from now, there will be a hardly a single cell in your body that exists today. Most of them will be brand new, a high proportion of these replaced and renewed many times over within that single year.

Our body is designed to last us an entire lifetime, and with care and nurturing it will do so. Sadly, there are very few of us (and I count myself firmly in the majority) who look after ourselves as well as we could. We eat foods that cause our body to work much harder than necessary in order to process them. We expose ourselves to toxins on a daily basis, whether voluntarily – through smoking, drugs and medicines or cosmetics, for example – or unconsciously (and usually unavoidably) through air and water born pollutants, chemical residues in the food that we eat (even in organic foods) or the materials our homes and offices are built from. We don't exercise enough so our joints stiffen, our muscles weaken and all our bodily systems grow sluggish. Our bodies can last us a lot longer than they currently do – a lot longer than we would dream to be possible – remaining fit and usable. It has been estimated that we could easily live to between 200 and 400 years old, if not more, leading useful and active lives for most of that time. If our bodies can renew themselves indefinitely – and there is no reason why they cannot – in theory they could last forever...

If this is the case then, why don't they? If each one of our body cells renews and replaces itself numerous times over the course of our lives, why don't we keep fit, healthy and in our prime throughout our lives? Why are the brand new cells born bearing the 'flaws' of the previous ones?

The answer is life. Or more specifically the unresolved, unreleased negative emotions, issues and fears that life instils in us. The most harmful attacks our bodies have to suffer are the mental and emotional ones. Stress is well-documented as a top 'body-wrecker'. Repressing emotions, not saying the things we need to say, holding on to past issues or burying and denying uncomfortable feelings and memories are just as destructive to our physical cells. These emotions are held in our bodies and transmitted into the memory of our cells, affecting their functioning and closing them down[1]. This cellular memory is them passed on to each new generation of replacement cells unless or until these 'causing' factors are released or the body dies. Louise Hay was a pioneer in the field of the Mind Body connection with her groundbreaking book *You Can Heal Your Life*[2] and there have been countless others since. All point to an (in my mind) irrefutable connection between our buried issues and our health. In *The Journey*[3], Brandon Bays tells the story of how she healed herself of a huge life-threatening tumour through uncovering and releasing buried past memories and emotions. The processes she was gifted created a blueprint for a healing process that has been successfully followed by thousands of people worldwide. This is a huge field in itself, well beyond the scope of this short sub-chapter, but for those readers wishing to delve further I have included some suggested reading at the end of the book. I firmly believe that working to release our deepest buried fears and damaging emotions is probably the most important thing we can do to lead a longer and healthier (and happier!) life. You can do this on your own – many of the books relating to this subject have their own processes and it's a case of discovering which works best for you – or you can visit one of the many registered therapists. I find that, for me, working with someone else is always more effective, as having them lead the process frees up my focus and allows me much deeper access to my inner wisdom. Interestingly, the principles behind this type of healing link in very closely to the steps to re-awakening our wings. All, at their foundation, are linked to releasing fear and all its related negative aspects so that we can forgive, let go and live in joy, love and acceptance.

We came into this world to embrace it, to live its delights and sate our curiosity. When we reconnect with our physicality, with being part of the physical world around us (which includes the people in it!), when we relearn how to revel in being in our bodies and in our sensuality, to balance our physical and spiritual needs, then we are fulfilling one of our main reasons for being here.

POWER THOUGHT
Stop...Breathe...Be...

Part III

WHERE DO WE GO FROM HERE?

A conversation

'*The world is changing. Humanity is evolving. Some are waking while others prefer to remain in their comatose sleep-walking existence. They think it is easier that way. The question is, which do you want to be?*

How do we wake up?
See, but see with your heart and Soul rather than your eyes. You are living a process that began decades ago and which will go on for many more to come; a process that is gradually re-aligning humankind's energy vibrations to a higher frequency.

What type of vibrations?
Spiritual energy. Thoughts. Emotions. Already people are opening up to these frequencies. They are working with Earth and cosmic energies, healing energies. They are opening to guidance and the Higher Realms. Their psychic senses are strengthening. For those who wish to see, all is possible.

And for those who don't?
It will be a difficult time for them. Change is always hardest for those who resist.

But we always have a choice. Can we not choose to stay asleep?
That is true. All do have that choice. But no matter how much you pull the covers back over your head, keep your eyes tightly shut and try to sleep once more, these changes are happening. They are a call from whence you came, a call to return to Source, reminding you of your forgotten connection.

Those who are determined to stay asleep will find their vibrations falling as they follow their current path, which will be longer and harder and may take them lower than they wish to go. But it must be so for it is only when they reach this darkness that they will choose to wake and seek the light.

* * *

We are currently experiencing a global shift in our mass consciousness as we move to the next stage of our spiritual evolution. One by one, we are remembering our wings and waking up to a new awareness and a desire to look beyond the obvious. Secret knowledge, once closely guarded and passed on only to the chosen few, is now available to everyone who wishes to hear it. Many keepers of ancient wisdom say they are receiving messages from their guiding spirits telling them that the time has come to share this information.

More and more people are remembering their wings and making their first tentative attempts to fly. They may be drawn to become healers, teachers or clairvoyants or just desire a new way of relating to life. A few give up at their first hesitant stumbles, while many more persevere, flying higher and higher, inspiring others to do the same.

This shift corresponds to a re-awakening and a re-recognition of the divine feminine, after the millennia when male energy dominated. It is no coincidence that a large number of the already awakened light-bringers are women who, like the wise women of the past, are spreading the wisdom of eternity into this transient physical world. They lead by example, wings joyfully unfurled, shining in the light. They are living their lives in the 'new' way, teaching through example.

This is not to denigrate or repress the masculine in its turn. Instead we are returning to a natural equilibrium where the masculine energies of action, assertiveness and logic are once more tempered by the feminine qualities of harmony, compassion and intuition . Yin and yang in perfect balance.

We have reached the end of this part of our journey but this ending is just a beginning. Once our wings begin to unfurl, new possibilities unfold before us, leading us in exciting and previously unseen directions. Go with life. Choose your dreams and let life carry you where it will in order to fulfil them. The voyage will amaze you.

Some closing thoughts

This is it. The end of my first book. As I'm writing these words I am also looking back over the 18 months since I began. It has been a long journey, occasionally frustrating, more often exciting and uplifting, and it has allowed me to grow beyond all my expectations. Forgotten Wings has been both a mirror and a teacher for me. When I was finding it hard to express things clearly, those were the areas I most needed to look at in my own life.

I am very aware that it wasn't only me writing. In fact it's probably fair to say my contribution was small. My fingers may have held the pen and tapped the keyboard, my mind may have organised the chapters and structure but much of the wisdom within came from a far deeper place. It is said that we teach that which we most need to learn. Well, I am eternally grateful to Source for providing me with such a wonderful and rewarding opportunity to further my own learning and growth.

As my understanding of myself, life and the reality beyond the illusion has deepened, so my own wings have grown stronger and brighter. I am filled with a powerful desire for change in my life and a lusty excitement at the prospect of stepping into the unknown, into the 'void of infinite possibilities'. At the time of writing these closing words, I have put my home on the market in order to follow more closely my heart and my dreams. To live my life the way life is intended to be lived. I have at last released the fear that held me back for so long. And I am so looking forward to the next stage in my journey.

References & end notes

Key 1

1. The Secret, Rhonda Byrne; Simon & Schuster Ltd, 2006
2. The Spontaneous Healing of Belief, Gregg Braden; Hay House, 2008
3. Ask & It is Given, Esther & Jerry Hicks; Hay House, 2005
4. The Secret, Rhonda Byrne; Simon & Schuster Ltd, 2006
5. Cosmic Order, Barbel Mohr; Mobius, 2006
6. for more information visit Gary Craig's highly informative website: www.emofree.com

Key 3

1. The Biology of Belief, Bruce Lipton PhD; Cygnus Books, 2005
2. Carl Jung

Key 4

1. taken from the poem *'Leisure'* by W H Davies

Key 5

1. for an interesting view on this read Neale Donald Walsch, What God Wants; Mobius, 2006
2. physicsworld.com; Jan 05

Key 6

1. The teachings of Abraham, a series of books based on the teachings of the non-physical beings known as Abraham; Esther & Jerry Hicks, Hay House (see suggested reading for specific titles)
2. A World Without Time, Palle Yourgrau; Penguin, 2005
3. Freedom Is, Brandon Bays; Hodder & Stoughton, 2006

Key 7

1 A World Without Time, Palle Yourgrau; Penguin, 2005

Key 9

1 The Divine Matrix, Gregg Braden; Hay House, 2007

Key 10

1 The Biology of Belief, Bruce Lipton; Cygnus Books, 2006
2 You Can Heal Your Life, Louise Hay; Hay House, 1984
3 The Journey, Brandon Bays; Thorsons 1999

Further reading & resources

Brandon Bays *The Journey* (Thorsons, 1999)

Gregg Braden *The Divine Matrix* (Hay House, 2007)

Deepak Chopra *Quantum Healing* (Bantam Press, 1989)

The Seven Spiritual Laws of Success (Bantam Press, 1996, HB)

Hale Dwoskin *The Sedona Method* ((Element, 2005)

Gill Edwards *Wild Love* (Piatkus, 2006)

Life is a Gift (Piatkus, 2007)

Dr Wayne Dyer *The Power of Intention* (Hay House, 2004)

Shakti Gawain *Living in the Light* (New World Library, 1998)

Louise Hay *You Can Heal Your Life* (Hay House, 1984)

Esther & Jerry Hicks *Ask and It Is Given* (Hay House, 2005)

The Incredible Power of Emotions (

Karen Kingston *Clear Your Clutter with Feng Shui* (Piatkus, 2008)

Loretta Laroche *Life is Short - Wear Your Party Pants* (Hay House, 2003)

Bruce Lipton *The Biology of Belief* (Cygnus Books, 2006)

Debbie Shapiro *Your Body Speaks Your Mind* (Piatkus, 2007)

Marci Shimoff *Happy For No Reason* (Free Press, 2009)

Sue Stone *Love Life, Live Life* (Hemmick press, 2007)

Neale Donald Walsch the *Conversations With God* series (Hodder Mobius)

Happier Than God (Hampton Roads Publishing Co, 2008)

What God Wants (Mobius, 2006)

Wallace D. Wattles *The Science of Getting Rich* (rev. Beyond Words Publishing, 2008)

Other resources

www.emofree.com *The* website for Emotional Freedom Technique. Masses of free information including 'How To' manuals

About the author

Dawn Henderson is a warm and inspiring writer, teacher and healer who began her spiritual voyage of discovery over 12 years ago when a friend introduced her to Reiki, which led to her eventual attunement as a Reiki Master. Since then she has trained in crystal healing, ThetaHealing™ and Reference Point Therapy. She is also a certified Louise Hay *Heal Your Life* workshop facilitator.

For several years Dawn's quest for a deeper spiritual connection and understanding has led her on a heart and soul awakening apprenticeship. Forgotten Wings is the result of an ever more powerful pull to share her wisdom and soul knowledge with others. She has a grounded, earthy spirituality based as much in the appreciation and enjoyment of our physical existence as in that of the invisible world around and within us.

Dawn has two grown up children and currently lives in the beautiful English county of Wiltshire. In addition to her passion for her own spiritual and personal growth, she loves dancing, gardening, working with herb and plant remedies and walking in the wilder areas of the UK countryside.

For information on Dawn and her work visit
www.dawnhenderson.co.uk

BOOKS

O is a symbol of the world, of oneness and unity. In different cultures it also means the "eye," symbolizing knowledge and insight. We aim to publish books that are accessible, constructive and that challenge accepted opinion, both that of academia and the "moral majority."

Our books are available in all good English language bookstores worldwide. If you don't see the book on the shelves ask the bookstore to order it for you, quoting the ISBN number and title. Alternatively you can order online (all major online retail sites carry our titles) or contact the distributor in the relevant country, listed on the copyright page.

See our website www.o-books.net for a full list of over 500 titles, growing by 100 a year.

And tune in to myspiritradio.com for our book review radio show, hosted by June-Elleni Laine, where you can listen to the authors discussing their books.

mySpiritRadio